Against Bourgeois Society by Johann Georg Eccarius
First Prism Key Press Edition 2012

Prism Key Press
New York, NY 10001
PrismKeyPress.com

ISBN-13: 978-1468139419

Against Bourgeois Society
The Selected Works of Johann Georg Eccarius

CONTENTS

The Last Stage of Bourgeois Society

The social and political development of mankind is a series of phases and stages, an unavoidable process through which the human race had to pass, and is perpetually passing, to arrive at a certain end.

Nations have arisen as it were from obscurity, they have been mighty and flourishing, and then passed to decline and ruin. At some particular periods war and anarchy have been so universal that the very existence of the human species has appeared to be at stake. Powerful empires have been swept from the face of the earth. The barbarians who have conquered and ruined them have carried the ruins and trophies to distant places and founded new empires. But though nations have been extinguished, exterminating wars and revolutions have taken place, the human race has survived them all, and has incessantly tended towards improvement and perfection. Every state of society that has been overthrown has furnished the material for the establishment of a succeeding one of a more progressive character: and every newly established state of society has been the necessary result of the preceding one. Every one, according to the degree of civilisation on which it was founded, has had its social and political organization, its religion and laws, its notions of justice; and every established system has at some particular period satisfied the wants of society, and corresponded with the claims that men made upon life.

Times of great commotions, anarchy, and revolutions, have always been the periods when the existing arrangements no longer answered the wants and necessities of the population. Whenever an existing state of things has ceased to satisfy the claims of society, the ruled have commenced to question the rights and authority of the rulers; men have questioned the propriety of their religion; society has begun to revolt; strifes, struggles, and battles have ensued between the oppressors and oppressed; and the ultimate result has been the dissolution of the old, and the establishment of a new, state of society.

Every new state of society has introduced its own peculiar mode of workship, one that has always been compatible with the mode of produce, with the manner in which the different tribes or nations of the different periods obtained their means of living. Thus the ancients had their gods and goddesses to whom they sacrificed a share of their acquisitions, consisting either of the fruits of the soil, or the booties of war and plunder. The feudal system (the mission of which was to compel savage and wandering tribes to settle in fixed habitations and pursue peaceable occupations in trade and agriculture, or to protect those who were already settled against the plunderings and ravages of their barbaric neighbours) had its "right divine," and its universal catholic church commanding blind and unconditional belief and obedience. Modern society, the state of free competition in art, science, trade, and industry, has its liberty of conscience, freedom of thought, and discussion, etc., in short, free competition in religious matters, and contemplations.

One of the principal features of all the changes that have yet taken place has been a change in the relations of property, from which all the social and political organizations have originated.

At all times when society has been revolutionized, the supporters of old systems, who had privileges and advantages over others, have prophesied that the world would be ruined if new systems were adopted. On the other side, those who happened to be the champions of progress, have imagined that their peculiar systems were the only true ones, that their principles were the only principles worth fighting for, that they were inherent in human nature, and if really established and administered would be an eternal source of happiness, making all future changes and revolutions unnecessary.

8

The same thing has been and is still repeated, over and over again. The men of the middle age accused the ancients of idolatry, and blamed their system of slavery. They proclaimed the emancipation of the slaves, and made the slaves of the Roman empire serfs and bond-men; forgetting at the same time that the ancient world had laboured for centuries to prepare the ground on which the feudal system could be erected. The modern bourgeoisie, the discoverers of the natural rights of men, have raved and are incessantly raving against feudalism, against serfdom, and bondage. They call it the age of anarchy and oppression; yet they have commenced business with the stock which they accumulated under the wings of feudalism; they have extended that knowledge and industry which they acquired under its protection; they have abolished serfdom and bondage for their own aggrandizement, and have created a numerous *proletariat*—modern slaves—who have to get a scanty subsistence by working for wages.

They have been mistaken; what they considered the natural rights of man were only the rights of men living in that particular state of society.

They have in their turn become as great tyrants as were the feudal Lords and Kings; and, like their predecessors, they have for their own security been compelled to create conditions under which not only a new progressive state of society is becoming possible, but compulsory.

Thus the bourgeoisie has fulfilled its mission in history, and no more.

It is true the accomplishments that have been made under the bourgeois *regime* surpass those of all former ages; but they could not have been made without having all the previous acquirements as a foundation for them. The declarations of our bourgeois politicians and economists that the essence of the present state of society is eternal, and that a deviation from it will lead to ruin and barbarism, are the more absurd, since the revolutionary volcano is continually threatening to swamp the whole system, and whatever they undertake to put a stop to, has only the effect of pouring oil on to the fire.

The events and commotions that have lately occurred are the most unmistakeable signs that the existing state of bourgeois society is in its last stage, and is verging towards ruin and dissolution. When our statesmen say that socialism and communism will lead to ruin, they are in so far right, as socialism and communism stipulate the annihilation of bourgeois society, its relations of property, its mode of appropriation, distribution, and *exploitation.* But mankind will not be ruined. Production and distribution will be freed from the shackles that are imposed upon them; they will not be dependent on the avidity, for gain, of some individuals, who are at present known under the denomination of "manufacturers," "merchants," "shopkeepers," etc., etc., for at present the lust of gain is the only stimulant to production, distribution, and exchange. The farmer does not cultivate the soil because society is in want of agricultural produce, but because the market price is higher than the cost of production. If society could not afford to pay that price, the farmer would abandon his land, though the majority of the people might die for the want of food. We read very often, indeed, complaints of low prices caused by over-production or abundant harvests, while in one and the same paper we read reports of people being utterly destitute of the necessaries of life. Times of disturbance and dissolution have generally been accompanied by a comparative amount of misery and destitution, for it is misery and destitution that drive the masses to revolt and rebellion. I say comparative, because the wants and necessaries of mankind vary with the degree of civilization. What a Russian serf would consider comfort, an English proletarian might deem misery.

There has been for some years past an amount of misery in existence which is continually increasing. The "Manchester school" politicians, and economists, have told us a great deal of late about "the comparative well-being of the working classes." By what standard do they compare this alleged well-being?

Why, by the standard of 1847—a time of universal stagnation in trade, with a famine into the bargain. A very strong argument indeed in favour of existing arrangements, that the working classes are better off in a year of unexampled prosperity than in a year of famine and commercial stagnation. Some weeks ago the *Economist* was highly gratified at the comparative well-being of the working classes, manifested in the increase of population and marriages during the last quarter. I very much doubt whether the increase of population and marriages, is in all cases, the result of well-being. Many a young couple join in holy matrimony, because their earnings do not enable them to live single. Their "issue," therefore, is not the result of well-being but of misery. With all the ostentatious boast of increasing trade and prosperity, our profit-mongers have not been able to reclaim more than 38,770 able-bodied paupers out of 166,828, from the 1st July 1848, till the same date 1850. On the 1st July last, society had still to keep 128,058 able-bodied paupers in the workhouses, in spite of "prosperity." Besides these there are hundreds of thousands who only get half a living, and prefer starving at home to going into workhouses.

The increase of friendly societies is also taken as a proof of increasing prosperity among the working-classes. Our Manchester politicians are greatly mistaken. The increase of friendly societies merely proves that the spare pennies of a great many are wanted to help one in case of need; and that working men are disgusted with applying for parish relief. The New Poor Law, and the cruel treatment of "in-door Paupers," do much toward increasing the number of friendly societies. They may as well tell us that our workhouses, our poor-law system, and our convict establishments, are emblems of the well-being of the working-classes. Without pauperism and crime, there would be no occasion for workhouses, poor-laws, and convict establishments. And without the wretchedness prevalent among the working-classes, there would be no occasion for societies for mutual relief and support.

Mr. Porter pretends to prove the wealth of the working-classes by the increase of the deposits in the Savings' Banks. He states that the amount of deposits in 1846 was in England, Wales, and Ireland, £ 29,669,384,—being equal to 24 s. per head,—while in 1821 the amount only averaged 12s. 8d. per head. I will not inquire how far these deposits belong to the working-classes, (the picture of pauperism just exhibited corresponds very badly), but whatever the amount belonging to working-men may be, it only shews that their earnings are not sufficient to invest them otherwise, and that their circumstances are so precarious that they are afraid to spend on luxuries and comfort that little of their income which is over and above their bare subsistence. Besides, the Savings' Banks are principally an accommodation for governments and the bourgeoisie.

Mr. Porter also attempts to disprove the position often assumed,—that the rich are becoming richer, and the poor poorer. He does so by shewing that the revenue liable to the income tax, has since 1812 increased nearly three-fold greater than the population during the same period. But Mr. Porter says nothing about the poor, whether their income has increased at the same ratio. According to his statement, the income of the bourgeoisie has increased something like five-fold. Allowing the population to be nearly double now what it was in 1812, if the income of the proletariat had increased in the same proportion, every working-man who had one pound a week, in 1812, ought to have two pounds ten shillings now. I beg Mr. Porter's pardon for maintaining that the income of the proletarian has rather shewn a tendency to decrease below the pound; and therefore Mr. Porter's figures prove nothing else but that the rich *are* becoming *richer,* and the poor *poorer.* The breach is becoming wider and wider; and the building must soon fall to the ground.)

Every state of society admits of certain improvements called reforms. These reforms are either required by the interest of the whole ruling class, or they are only for the benefit of a particular fraction. In the former case they are carried without much agitation; in the latter, that fraction for whose benefit they are to be carried, call themselves reformers; these form a distinct party, and appeal to the oppressed (they call it to the nation) to aid them in their endeavours.

If the object to be achieved is a political one, like the Reform Bill, the franchise and other good things are promised, and the poor are drawn into the agitation. When the object is gained, the alliance is abandoned, generally from above, and the concessions made to the allies below, are so curtailed, as to amount to something like nothing at all. If the reform is merely of an economical character, other baits are held out to the oppressed, such as "a big loaf;" but at the time of the anti-corn-law league, the fish, though hungry, wouldn't bite.

Such reforms, however, are generally carried when the whole government machinery appears to be at a stand-still, and when the oppressed are threatening to attack the state.

The reformers, at such times, point at the imminent danger that would arise from further resistance; thus they frighten the conservative fraction to surrender. If the oppressed have a demand for their own particular class-interest, and are sufficiently organized to agitate for it, these bit by bit reforms become really conservative measures, since the execution of them deprives the extreme party of the chance to animate that part of the body politic, who side with every thing in the shape of reform, and who are generally indifferent to political matters as long as they have got a crust to gnaw at. Whenever such a reform is carried, peace is restored, the machinery of the state gets again in motion, and all seems well. This restoration of peace, however, is of short duration. Hostilities are not abolished, they are only suspended, and soon recommence. The most progressive fraction of the ruling class is again compelled to propose reforms, which are the more extensive and energetic, as the time of dissolution is drawing nearer. These reformers generally pretend that a real radical reform would set all things right, and prevent further disturbances and agitation. Of course these reforms are all to be carried by "legal and constitutional means!" But however extensive and radical these reforms may be, they alter nothing in the fundamental system of an existing state of things. They only remove grievances, which are impediments to that very state of society, within which they are carried out. Therefore one of the reforms must be the last one, beyond which there is no possibility of reforming without changing the state of things entirely.

Our present state of society is one that will not admit of much further "reform." The reform scheme, which is at present occupying the public mind, and which will arouse the official John Bull at the next crisis, is the last one that can be carried out without laying the destroying axe to the root of bourgeois society. All the improvements that may be carried out within the existing state of society in England, are comprised in Parliamentary and Financial Reform; beyond this there is no alternative.

That fraction of the bourgeoisie, who have made it their special mission to carry out this scheme, have not failed to represent it as comprising the interest of the whole nation. They appeal to the nation in general, and to the proletariat in particular, to aid them in their struggle. The franchise, education, plenty of work and good wages are promised; but the cloven-foot peeps through everywhere, and the proletarians are accordingly very backward with their co-operation. The Manchester politicians are honest enough to tell us, as a matter of course, that the money price of labour will go down, when provisions become cheaper; but they add that "the real recompense will rather increase than diminish." They show how comfortable we might be, if we would but abstain from drinking spirits, and the indulgence of other "sensual gratifications." Our present income, they say, will admit of plain and substantial living and how graceful (!!!) they allow us to spend six pence per week, in "good, useful, and cheap literature," such as the cotton lords choose to furnish through the medium of "John Cassel's library," that we may get a true (?) knowledge of the factory system, and the injurious consequences (?) of the Ten Hours' Bill! Education is set forth as a prime necessary of life (and I am convinced it really is), but as far as it is promoted by the Manchester school, with regard to the working classes, it merely means that if we received a good education in the true Manchester principles, we would come to the belief that we have no reason to grumble about our lot. The same benefactors of the working class, tell us that if we only would be parsimonious, we could save many a shilling. As the best means for investing our savings, they advise us to join the freehold land societies, and purchase a vote, that we may vote for a Financial Reform candidate at the next election. Mr. Cobden seems to be rather grieved that the wages slaves do not avail themselves of the opportunity of purchasing a freehold and a vote, "for (as he said at the London Tavern) half the money spent in gin would win all the counties." What a pity that working-men won't listen to advice.

Now with regard to parliamentary reform, and the pretended concessions made in the programme of the National Reform Association; before we believe that these concessions are made for us, we must investigate them, and enquire whether the parliamentary reformers are really in want of our co-operation or not. The little Charter contains no concession to the working classes. Those points which appear as such at first sight, are so necessary, and so useful to the Manchester school, that they can scarcely do without them. The qualification of electors, set forth in the first paragraph is a tax qualification: hence money not the man would be the elector. The second point, vote by ballot, is necessary for rescuing the farmers and little tradesmen from the control of the aristocracy. The shortening of the duration of Parliament, is compatible with the interest of mill-owners. An equalisation of the electoral districts, according to the population, is the only means by which the manufacturers can send a majority of financial reformers into

15

the House of Commons. It is the medium through which the supremacy of the industrial bourgeois is to be legally established, and the influence of the aristocracy in the legislature paralysed. The last point, "no property qualification for members of parliament," which has been particularly proclaimed as a concession to the proletariat is without the payment of members not worth a straw to the working classes; while for the profit-mongers it is exceedingly useful. By means of this point the mill-owners could manage to have a host of their scribes, lecturers, *Chartist renegades,* and other humble servants returned, who might be called on duty whenever their masters required their aid in the house. Such are the concessions of the National Reform Association!

To working-men the most essential point of the programme is the qualification of electors. As it stands in the programme of the "Reformers" it certainly seems as if it would put a vote within the reach of many a workingman; but before it can become the law of the land it will have to go through parliament, where it will be shaped in such a manner as to deprive the working class of the chance of returning even a small number of representatives, whose principles might be antagonistic to the rule of capital. Then, the little Chartists will lament, on public platforms, that the five points have not been carried in their original integrity; but for the sake of legality they will advise us to put up with the new "reform," and be satisfied that we have defeated the aristocratic foe, in some measure. A mutilation, in which those pretended Chartists will concur, can thus be attributed to aristocratic hostility and arrogance!

Our bourgeois progressists, in England, are too well versed in political economy; they understand their own class-interest and the antagonism between labour and capital too well to entertain such foolish notions as the republican ideologists across the channel, who believe that universal suffrage is compatible with the rule of capital. They are fully aware that even a strong proletarian opposition in parliament would be injurious, if not fatal, to their interest; hence, for the sake of their own preservation, they will be compelled to withold the franchise from workingmen as much as possible.

The end of parliamentary reform is, to make the supremacy of the manufacturing interest the law of the land. Though for the last twenty years all vital questions have been decided in favour of that interest, and the mill-owners have, in fact, ruled the destinies of the empire, yet there is no legal guarantee for their supremacy. By the existing constitution of the House of Commons, the nobles have not only the means of strongly resisting the measures of their rivals, but they have the legal power to reject them altogether. Hence, the mill-owners, who consider themselves the sole benefactors of society, have, to their great annoyance, either to beg the nobles to consent to their measures, or to frighten them into consent by agitations. To avoid this humiliation and trouble they must establish their supremacy by law, *i. e.* they must paralyse the political power of the aristocracy, and make themselves masters of the legislature; they must conquer the constitution.

In order to achieve this conquest, only one point of the programme needs to be executed, that is, the equalisation of the electoral districts. According to the present state of constituencies, 353 more or less conservative members are returned by little more than 227,000 electors, the remaining 297 by something above 823,000 electors. Again, 25 of the smallest constituencies with 9,153 electors, return 50 members, while 25 of the largest with 229,365 electors, return also 50 members. An equalisation of the electoral districts would produce the following results:—The 297,000 electors, who at present return 23 members more than a clear majority, would return something like 141 members; and the 823,000 electors would return 509 members. The 25 smallest constituencies would return 5 members, while the 25 largest would return 142. Thus we see that an equalisation in the electoral districts would completely swamp the protectionist, and other more or less conservative constituencies, without a single elector being added to the present register; and the aristocracy would lose all power and influence in the House of Commons. Now with regard to an extension of the suffrage, vote by ballot, and no property qualification for members; these are mere measures of convenience, which, of course, will add to the success of the scheme. But even if the number of electors should be increased 50 per cent., which would be an additional number of about 525,000, very few of the working men would get a vote, except such as are "good boys" and have no political opinion of their own.

The Friend of the People. No.6, 18 January 1851

It is beyond doubt that the bourgeois reformers neither want an extensive alteration in the constitution, nor the co-operation of the proletarians as a class, for the accomplishment of their "reform". Indeed, an ally like the proletariat, whose social position is so entirely antagonistic to that of the bourgeoisie, must be very dangerous. But as the little chartists are all known to be practical men, who are not likely to take much trouble about things which cannot be turned into hard cash, they must have some reason for their big-hearted generosity in proposing to extend the franchise to working-men, etc. The reason is obvious. They are afraid of proletarian ascendancy, and their pretended concession to the working-class is merely a lure by which they endeavour to entrap the proletarian lion, lest he might do mischief to the profit-mongers' cause. As the bourgeois is in the habit of having all his work done, and fortunes heaped up, by the proletarian, so he expects, whenever he is at variance in politics with his aristocratic com-rogue, that the wages-slave should fight it out, and leave the spoils of victory to his master. Whether the great bulk of the working-class will answer this expectation in the coming struggle the future will tell.

The promises of pecuniary advantage, ease, and comfort to the working-classes, resulting from financial reform are equally fallacious. Why do our manufacturers agitate for financial reform and direct taxation? Because they have an interest in having their work done at the cheapest rate, and employ as few men as possible. The government is no more than a committee, who manage the collective affairs of the bourgeoisie.

The ministers, and all the minor government officers, stand in the same relation to the bourgeoisie as the directors, and minor servants of a railroad company, stand to the shareholders. It is, therefore, the interest of the bourgeoisie to make government affairs as simple as possible, to employ as few men as possible, and pay as little as possible. Indirect taxation is one of the complicated affairs which requires a great number of men, who consume a considerable part of the gross revenue. Besides this, many, who under a system of direct taxation would have to contribute a considerable part towards defraying the expenses of the state, are comparatively low taxed, and finally it makes the revenue of the state very uncertain, and enhances the price of food. A heavy budget makes a great part of the capital of a country unproductive. A great amount of capital remains in the hands of stock-jobbers without producing anything, merely going out of one pocket into another; this makes it difficult for the manufacturer to borrow money; it also enhances the rate of interest on capital. The taxes which the working people have to pay in the price of their food must be paid by the employers in the form of wages. All this is against the interest of the manufacturers. The interests of manufacturers require that the budget should be at the minimum, because there would be less chance for heavy loans, and the stock-jobbers would be obliged to lend their money to manufacturers at a low rate of interest. Food should not pay taxes of any kind, then the workmen could work cheaper, and the manufacturer would be better able to compete with the foreign rival who must be undersold in his own home market.

As the improvement and increase of the productive powers, particularly of machinery, has made considerable progress in foreign countries, it has become imperative to the

English manufacturers to produce and sell their goods at a much lower price. To accomplish this, all commercial impediments, financial grievances, etc., must be abolished; every shilling that can be made productive must be turned to account. Of the collective bourgeoisie there is but one fraction whose interest is at variance with the general interest of the class, the fundholders and stock-jobbers, whose speculations will be greatly diminished by financial reform. All the rest, be they farmers, merchants, or manufacturers, can no longer suffer a profligate aristocracy to enjoy pensions and sinecures for nothing. They can no longer allow an extravagant priesthood to waste twelve millions annually to no purpose. They cannot tolerate a dissipating system of government with such a complicated system of taxation like the present, where there are so many chances of finding situations and places for friends and favourites, who form a host of idle and mischievous retainers.

The growth of English industry demands that the affairs of government be made pure and simple; that royalty should be stripped of all the remnants of barbarism pressing heavily on the public purse.

The next commercial stagnation will, no doubt, frighten whigs and tories, beefeaters, stock-jobbers, and fund-holders to surrender, and the radical reformers will begin their sway. But will their "radical reforms" change the fundamental system of bourgeois society? Certainly not. The fundamental system of bourgeois society is the rule of capital, and the consequent antagonism between labour and capital, between the wages-slave and the capitalist, between the working poor and the sluggish rich. Parliamentary, financial, and all the bourgeois reforms, will not ameliorate these hostile relations in the slightest degree; on the contrary, they will rather aggravate them.

The reforms, however sweeping and radical, do in reality, only strip bourgeois society of the feudal and barbarous ornaments inherited from the middle age. They are, therefore, for the advantage and preservation of the ruling class.

All the pompous speeches at ticket and public meetings are mere humbug with regard to the working classes. The interest of the capitalist, his mode of accumulating wealth, in short, the entire state of society, is at stake at every moment that industry fails to afford sufficient to the working classes to prolong their slavish existence. As the dissolution of the existing state of society is tantamount to the emancipation of the working millions, the working classes are interested in promoting it as speedily as possible. If, therefore, financial reform really will afford some ease and comfort to the working classes, they will not receive it as a favour from the hands of the bourgeois reformers, but merely as a means by which the latter will endeavour to impose quietness upon the former. But what will be the general results of financial reform and direct taxation? If a competition, more or less limited, has hitherto tended to create a revolutionary proletariat, can it be imagined that when commerce and industry shall be freed from all fetters, it will be less effective in the same direction? By no means. Who are the chief supporters of royalty and government at present? The beef-eaters, the pensioners, the sinecurists, the stock-jobbers, the fund-holders, the numerous government and church officials, and place-men; above all, the standing army. These again command the support of all the little tradesmen and shopkeepers with whom they deal. Let them do away with pensioners and sinecurists, let them reduce the fund-holders and government officials, let them separate the church from the state, and all these parties, with their dependant tradesmen, have no longer an interest in supporting the government. Let them reduce or abolish the standing army, and they will abandon the weapons by means of which they impose their laws upon society. But then it will be said there will be no cause to grumble when all these grievances are removed. When once parliamentary and financial reform is carried, royalty and government will be stripped of all their aristocratic and feudal splendour and retainers; and our bourgeois grumblers will lose the chance of laying all the causes of social misery and degradation to the account of a wicked and profligate aristocracy; the curtains will be removed, behind which the tyranny of the capitalists is partly hidden. The rule of capital will appear clearly before the light of day, and its tyrannical character will be recognised by even the indifferent and the ignorant. Thus, while the interest of the bourgeoisie demands that their own government must be reduced to its simplest form, they are obliged to deprive it of the main pillar of its stability, and reduce it to that level on which it can be conquered by the proletariat.

The power of merchants and manufacturers consists in the amount of capital at their disposal, and in the amount of commodities which they can purchase or command.

Therefore, whatever increases their capital, or tends to reduce the price of commodities, must increase their power, and hasten competition. When indirect taxation comes to be abolished, the trading capital of the merchants and manufacturers will increase to the extent of the amount of commodities purchased for the same money. For instance, the same amount of money which brings one cwt. of tea or tobacco to market now, will bring four cwts. when the tax is taken off, consequently the power of those who deal in these articles, or their command over social products will increase four-fold. If the consumption of these articles does not increase proportionably, part of the capital now invested in the tea and tobacco trades must go into other channels, and increase competition and speculation. If no opportunity offers for investing the surplus capital in other speculations, the wholesale merchants will employ it in the retail trade, and become to the little tea-dealer what Moses and Nichol are to the honourable tailor, that is, the workers of his ruin.

The power of manufacturers will increase in proportion as labour and the raw material get cheaper. An actual reduction in the budget will increase their productive capital, and facilitate their credit. The inevitable result of all this will be over-production, mad speculations, industrial and commercial panics, which will far exceed all former convulsions of a like character.

The wages of labour will follow the same course as they have hitherto done. As the "reform" measures are not likely to be carried at any other time than in that of commercial stagnation, wages will come very near to a direct taxation level before ever these beneficial measures come into operation. The reduction of manual labour will do the rest.

But there is one particular set of operatives and tradesmen in this metropolis who will feel the blessings of "financial reform" more than any other in the United Kingdom. These are the operatives and little tradesmen of the west-end whose welfare depends on the aristocracy, pensioners, sinecurists, and officers in the army and navy. Any one who is acquainted with business at the west-end, knows that the principal customers of tradesmen and shopkeepers, are nobles, officers, and aristocratic retainers of government. These folks pay high prices, and run up large bills. They live like improvident workmen who spend their week's earnings before Saturday comes, and are always in debt. If the pensions, etc., are taken from them they will lose their credit, and the tradesmen their customers.

If the already much encumbered aristocracy lose the chance of putting their younger sons in the army, and other lucrative situations, and pay taxes into the bargain, they will be obliged to be more parsimonious in the expenditure of their revenues, the prosperity of the west-end shopocracy will be at an end, and the loyal "special constables" of 1848 will get into a rather precarious position. Thus, what hitherto could not be accomplished, will perhaps succeed under a Manchester school administration, i.e., to make London, and particularly the west-end (the most reactionary corner in the kingdom) a centre of political agitation and revolutionary movement.

We see that parliamentary and financial reform will produce none of the beneficial effects so largely predicted by the free traders.

It will neither change the antagonistic relations between labour and capital, nor permanently ameliorate the condition of the suffering millions. The material advantages that are promised to the working classes are illusory, for they will vanish before the labouring population can take possession of them. The real importance of the movement consists in the fraud and illusion it carries into certain democratic regions. The joy of the conquest, as far as the working classes are concerned, will last until they find that illusion and enthusiasm do not fill their stomachs, then they will get sober, and look at things as they really are. However, as I have already stated, whenever these financial grievances shall be removed, there will be no more chance of leading the oppressed astray, and concealing the real foe behind pompous speeches and false promises.

As far as the reform scheme will clear the battle field of rubbish, behind which some interest opposed to the labour-interest might be concealed, it is to our advantage to help the reformers into office. *But neither as allies, nor as friends, only as foes.* If we co-operate with them, we give all command of the course to be pursued, into their hands, we submit to their dictatorship, and whenever they chose to stop short we must stop too. As friends or allies we can only form the tail of a deceitful and treacherous head, and whenever this head choses to stop it must put the tail into confusion, and when the field would be ready for us, we should find ourselves disorganised. This is precisely what the little Chartists would like to see. If, on the contrary, we help as foes, and have a good organisation for our own class-interests, we can drive them farther than they wish to go themselves. We have an interest to get them into office, because that is the only favourable ground on which we can conquer them. In defeating the most progressive fraction of the bourgeoisie in office, we defeat the whole host. It is, therefore, important that the working classes should be well organised for their own party purposes; that they may be ready to attack their antagonists the moment their bill is carried, then we may force them to make some concessions. Besides, a good proletarian agitation would induce the conservatives much sooner to surrender, since they would look upon the proposed parliamentary and financial reform as a conservative measure compared with the charter and something more, which must soon follow the triumph of bourgeois "reform."

The Well-being of the Working Classes

During the last two years the eulogisers and apologists of the present system have been incessantly revelling on account of the success of our recently adopted commercial policy. Every new return of the revenue, of imports and exports, etc., was an improvement compared with the preceding one—a new sign of prosperity and increasing wealth. The recorders of profitmongering called triumphantly upon reactionary and revolutionary antagonists to behold the figures, and with an air of glorious self-satisfaction, they told the world that the rule of capital, free competition, and private enterprise, as at present existing, was the only true road to happiness.

During the same period, the contributors to the bourgeois press have taken especial care to intermix their cheerful reports with more or less detailed accounts of the working-man's happy condition, his lot has been painted with the most beautiful colours, and his well-being has given universal satisfaction to the defenders of the existing state of things.

Why is it that our oppressors have paid so much attention to this theme? Is it because of the love they bear to the wages-slave, as a human being and a fellow-creature? No! It is because they are sure of their prey as long as the working-man has a bone to pick and a crust to knaw.

Save the agents and instruments of sport and prostitution, the capitalist employs nobody, and pays no wages, unless he can make a profit out of it, and add to his wealth. Is it, therefore, wonderful that the wages-slave, the creator of commodities, should be a little more at ease in a period of unexampled prosperity, than in times of stagnation? But, it is asserted, in the face of numerous exposures of misery, wretchedness, and oppression, that the working classes are really well off—better than at any former period. To demonstrate this blessed state of felicity, the political economists have recourse to the returns of pauperism, the cheapness of food, etc., but they take good care never to mention the actual amount of wages received by the workman.

It is a fact, generally understood, that the wants of man —aye! and of the working-man too, vary with the degree of civilisation under which he exists. The standard of well-being is therefore *relative.* Well-being, in a civilised state of society, does not consist in the actual amount of commodities which an individual does consume, and command: it consists in the relative amount, that is—how far he partakes of the annual produce of the land and labour of his country, in *the proportion of his share to the gross revenue of the society of which he is a member.* The upholders of the present system ignore this, and take a positive standard. Anything above starvation level to the sons of toil they consider well-being. A working-man's condition may, according to their doctrine, be positively better than at any former period; while, at the same time, his relative *position is worse than ever—so* that he is really cheated.

Suppose that a certain nation, at a particular period, produces by its annual labour a gross revenue of £400,000,000. That, under this state of things, the amount of wages paid to the workmen of all descriptions, from the government clerk down to the street-sweeper, would average £50 each, and that this sum would enable the working man to live, and propagate his race, and make him contented with his lot.

Suppose, now, that during a space of fifty years the population had doubled, the money-value of the gross annual produce had also doubled, but that it had quadrupled in quantity, so that the working man could now purchase as much for £50 as formerly for £100. If his money wages had continued the same, his condition would be improved one hundred per cent; his command over the necessaries and luxuries of life would be doubled; his *relative position* would be the same.

Let us now suppose that during this period the invention

28

and improvement of machinery had been rapidly progressing; that the consequent diminution of manual labour had reduced its nominal price twenty-five per cent., and that the loss of time occasioned by slack time and a super-abundance of hands, had caused another decrease of fifteen per cent. per annum, we should find the working-man with £30 a-year at the expiration of this period.

Taking the amount of commodities purchased for £50 at the beginning of this period, to be equal to £100, the purchases made with £30, at the expiration would be equal to £120. Joseph Hume would call this an increase of real wages of twenty per cent. Yet, despite the positive increase of twenty per cent, the working man's relative income would be diminished *forty per cent.,* since his share ought to be equal to £200, to obtain his former proportion.

Thus, within the space of fifty years, the real income of the working-class, their command of social products, would have increased twenty per cent., while that of the capitalists would not only have increased one hundred per cent., on account of the progress in production, but they would have received an additional augmentation correspondent with the diminution of the relative income of the working class.

Such is our actual position in the blessed year of prosperity, 1851.

The contrast between labour and capital is hourly widening; the relation between the poor and the rich becomes daily more antagonistic; the more production is facilitated and augmented, the faster wealth is accumulated—the lower sink the working classes in the social scale.

But this is not all. Fifty years ago, the notions of what constitutes human life were very different from those of the present day. With the general progress of art and science, our views have expanded; with the increase of production, our wants have multiplied. We create manifold luxuries and comforts of life—they are continually exposed to our view—we are haunted in the streets with tickets and advertisements announcing places of amusement, and sales of articles of which we are in want. The trading capitalists themselves are the instigators of all this; every scheme that can be devised to draw a penny out of our pockets is eagerly seized upon; yet, when we complain of receiving too little for our toil, the whole chorus turns round and charges us with sensuality and extravagance. They have forced us to become politicians, to help them to fight out their quarrels with the aristocracy; and, having now become politicians for our own class-interest, they call us bloodthirsty ruffians, incendiaries, and anarchists. For profit's sake they have caused newspapers, periodicals, books, and pamphlets to be manufactured for us to read, and having arrived at conclusions unfavourable to their class interests, they accuse us of being visionary schemers. In the midst of civilization, surrounded by wealth and luxuries, with increased wants and knowledge, they imagine that we ought to be contented with the commonest necessaries of life, sleep, and hard-work, like our predecessors. Not to mention the idea which widely pervades the working classes, as to whether any individual ought to be permitted to exercise any private control whatever over the produce of other men's labour, our wants, in the present subordinate position, have increased fully one hundred per cent, during the last half century, while our means to satisfy them have only increased twenty per cent.

Moreover this is only the condition of the more favourably situated among the working-men. There are hundreds of thousands of good workmen, sober, and willing to work, who, for want of employment, are often without the most indispensable necessaries of physical life, even in the present time of prosperity and cheap food.

But even this is not all. As long as a working man is capable of keeping a lodging and a few sticks, though he may have bad work, or sometimes none at all—though he and his family should frequently be obliged to go without their proper meals, yet he is still considered as a member of society—he exists in the world of the living-he can communicate and mix with his fellow working men—and may occasionally enjoy an hour of happiness. Though his condition is a degraded one, he can sink still lower in the social scale—he can lose all, his precarious little comfort, his last vestige of independence—he can become a pauper, and be excluded from all family and social intercourse—with one word he can be shut up in the bastile of degradation.

Grievous and hard as it is for men who have wasted all their labour power, their strength, and energy of youth and manhood, to end their lives in the workhouse—yet it is infinitely harder and more grievous for adult able-bodied men to be excluded even from that little which is granted to the working man, and in the prime of life linger away in the workhouse virtually imprisoned.

As the exports of British and Irish produce and manufacture are generally taken as the thermometer for ascertaining the temperature of British commerce and manufacture, it is obvious that our foreign trade greatly influences trade in general, and consequently rules, to a certain extent, the demand for, and the price of, labour. Hence the fate of the British operative depends on the power and inclination of the Chinese, Americans, Germans, etc., to purchase our manufactures, and crime and pauperism increase and diminish in proportion as exports rise or fall.

The man who commits crime from want of food, and the pauper who goes to the workhouse to obtain relief, belong virtually to the same category of working-men; the only difference between the two is, that the former will not give himself up to imprisonment until he is overpowered by the arms of the law and police, while the latter submits quietly, and steps into the bastile. Both are driven into their respective confinement by the rule of capital. But, as it is not our intention to treat of criminals here, we shall content ourselves with the latter category of our unfortunate fellow-beings.

The number of adult able-bodied human beings doomed to subsist by parish support was, in—

590 unions, Jan. 1, 1849 – 201,644.

606 unions, Jan. 1, 1850 – 181,159.

---------------------- 1851 – 154,525.

The exports of British and Irish produce and manufacture during the same period amounted to £48,946,395 in 1848, £58,910,883 in 1849, and £65,756,032 in 1850. Thus, an increase of exports of £9,964,488 redeemed above 20,000 persons from pauperism in 1849, and a further increase of exports of £6,845,149 redeemed 26,634 persons in 1850.

These results have given complete satisfaction to the capitalists. They have put forth these figures as if the occasional decrease of pauperism was something heretofore unknown; yet the same thing has occurred over and over again. For years past the history of trade and commerce has been a continual rising and falling; the periodic recurrence of commercial crises has been as regular as the rising and setting of the sun. Will they tell us that pauperism must vanish because of free-trade? Look at the figures: to redeem the total number of adult able-bodied paupers would, under the present system, require an additional increase of our foreign trade of £50,000,000 annually. Will either our free-trade policy or the promised parliamentary and financial reform, enable our foreign customers to buy nearly twice as much of our goods as they do now? No!

Already, in spite of a deficient cotton crop and high priced raw material, the markets abroad are glutted with the finer descriptions of our cotton goods; and raw cotton having now become cheap, on account of an abundant harvest, our manufacturers are busily at work to over-stock the markets with heavy goods also. Besides, there is a general dullness in almost all branches of trade; and while the imports of raw material and colonial produce are heavy, the demand and prices decline. This and the late failures show that we have already arrived at the eve of another crisis, when pauperism again will increase until, after much ruin and misery, the next tide of prosperity sets in.

Thus we see there is no hope for those who linger away in the bastile, of being finally released under the existing system. Even in times of unexampled prosperity a considerable number of able-bodied men must be kept in unwilling idleness —and why? Is it because the people are too well housed, too well clad, and too well fed? or is it because there is no waste land that could be cultivated—no raw material to work with, etc.? No! it is because the drones of society have all they want, and to employ more productive labour might interfere with the profits of the capitalists.

There is no getting out of the dilemma without a complete change of system. Even if our home, as well as foreign, trade could be increased sufficiently to employ all hands at remunerative wages, the invention and improvement of machinery would soon restore the old conditions. Scarcely has famine and emigration reduced the hosts of Irish labourers, who used to migrate through the length and breadth of this country during the hay and harvest seasons, taking work almost at any price, and, therefore, keeping down wages,—ere reaping-machines came in from different quarters, and, at once, not only blight the hopes of the agricultural labourers to raise their wages, but even threaten to deprive them altogether of the little extra payment which they hitherto received in the harvest season.

On the other hand the reaping machine, together with other inventions and improvements, will relieve the farmers more and more from the necessity of employing an extraordinary number of hands during the summer months, which it has been their interest to keep (though it should be in the workhouse) in the rural districts. The services of these hands having become entirely useless, they will be driven to factory towns, still more to increase the surplus of the labour-seeking population, which again must tend to reduce wages.

Another fact, which demonstrates the precarious position of the working classes, is, that, even in times of unexampled prosperity, when the demand for labour has reached its maximum, the rate of wages cannot be maintained. There is scarcely any one branch of trade in which the capitalists have not attempted, and, alas! too frequently successfully, to reduce wages within the last two years. Such having been the case when trade was flourishing, what will it be under less favourable circumstances?

Such, then, is the social position of the modern wages-slaves; such the highly-praised condition which the apologists of the present system have the audacity to denominate *the real wel-being of the working classes*. If we could be induced to believe them, when perusing their pages, the pinching of the stomach, our attire, our lodgings, etc., would very soon remind us that we were grossly belied. If social progress, improvement of condition, and the well-being of the working classes, mean, that the more fortunate of working men shall advance one step to every hundred advanced by the capitalists, and the less fortunate toilers be trampled in the dust—if it mean that the producers of all wealth have no claim to participate in the enjoyment of the comforts and luxuries they create,—if it mean annihilation to some, hard work and privation to all,—then our antagonists are perfectly right. But the working man has different notions of well-being: the ages of spiritual delusion are past—we live in an age of materialism; the poor do not now rejoice in the splendour of their rich oppressors, as in times gone by; nor do they believe the superiority of the ruling classes to be of divine origin, or their own misery ordained by a supernatural power— and nothing short of a full share of the fruits of labour will satisfy their claims in the long run.

A Working Man's Refutation of Some Points of Political Economy Endorsed and Advocated by John Stuart Mill

II. Capital—Its Formation and Accumulation.

In my last I endeavoured to point out under what peculiar circumstances the prerequisites of production are capital. But there is both a history and a theory of capital. The former is generally ignored by middle class economists; the latter, with them, is the theory of confusion, errors, and sophistry. In the material sciences men commenced with things as they found them, dissolved them into their component parts, and gradually ascertained their origin. The professors of political economy, on the contrary, took things as they found them for granted; left the origin of capital to take care of itself; invented some specious theory respecting its existence and workings, and all the money-making public cried "Amen!" Had they, like modern geologists do the rocks, dissolved capital into its component parts, they would have arrived at conclusions different to those they have arrived at. They would not have met with so much applause at the hands of the magnates of modern society had they followed this course, they would rather have had to encounter their hostility as those who are not satisfied with writing apologetic eulogies upon the existing state of things, but dive deeper into the matter have to do; but political economy would have become a science under their hands, instead of a handmaid of the ruling classes. The origin of capital is the division of labour. As long as the division of labour was confined to the patriarchal and feudal family, capital was not formed and was not required. When the division of labour into separate and organized trades superseded the division of labour in the family, intermeddlers established themselves to distribute some of the produce of other people's labour. In the transit from the producer to the consumer a certain amount of this produce stuck to their fingers which they accumulated. In due course of time money making, buying and selling, became the aim of production. Those who had appropriated and accumulated the produce of other people's labour found themselves hampered and impeded by the guild and corporation laws, which required personal and technical, not wealth owning qualifications, to carry on the business of production. The so-called moneyed interest burst these fetters which had been forged to insure a subsistence to the handicraft man, to convert the runaway serf into a free citizen. They were regulations which were only compatible with a production that was for the most part calculated to supply local wants. The enriched intermeddler required a world for his market, and labourers who had either to do his bidding or die of starvation. He furnished the material which he had accumulated out of the past labour of others, and the most needy had to work them up on his own premises under his immediate control. Thus the division of labour was carried into the workshop, the produce of labour became the exclusive property of the employer, the labourer, the producer, became an appendage to, instead of an agent in, the process of production, buying and selling, exchange value, money-making became the aim of production. So much for the history of capital, now for the theory.

"Parsimony," says Adam Smith, "is the immediate cause of the increase of capital." "Capital is the result of saving," says Mr. Mill. What the father of political economy stated a hundred years ago is repeated in other words by the would-be Adam Smith of the nineteenth century, *the man of new ideas*. Had capitalist production, modern industry, not advanced by more rapid strides than her votaries—those who profess to explain her workings, and to trace the path upon which she is to proceed—it is a dead certainty that journeymen tailors would not be able to publish articles on political economy in working men's papers. Mr. Mill in his sophistical reasoning assumes that abstinence is the foundation of the accumulation of capital. Let us pause to examine this theory. If the man whose income is 50,000*l.* a year is content to live upon 25,000*l.*, he will have 25,000*l.* to dispose of as capital the following year. He thus abstains from consuming 25,000*l.* which he might have done. So far so good. But how does he get the 50,000*l.*? By his own exertions! It never happened. Mr. Mill, again repeating Adam Smith, says: —"Everything which is produced is consumed, both what is saved and what is said to be spent; and the former quite as rapidly as the latter. When people talk of the ancient wealth of a country, of riches inherited from ancestors, and similar expressions, the idea suggested is, that the riches so transmitted were produced long ago, at the time when they are said to have been first acquired. The fact is otherwise. The greater part, in value, of the wealth now existing in England has been produced by human hands within the last twelve months." How then can capital be the result of saving? How does it happen that one man gets 50,000*l.* worth out of the produce of one year's labour? According to Professor Leone Levi's estimate, which I have no reason either to question or endorse, the average earnings of adult male labourers in England is 58*l.* 10s. a year. The man with 50,000*l.* therefore gets 1,030 times as much as the labourer. I have nearly forty years of business experience in villages, small towns, and large towns, and different countries, but I never found that a quick and industrious man could, under equal facilities, earn twice as much as a slow and lazy one. But here is a man getting one thousand and thirty times as much as the average labourer. It may be objected that the intellectual labour of direction and superintendence deserves a higher remuneration. We do not know that the 50,000*l.* man directs and superintends. How intellectual labour is remunerated, unless a man is in keeping with certain parties and becomes a bishop or a lord chancellor, we all know. The men who are engaged to direct and superintend may get five, ten, even twenty times as much as a good skilled workman and then it will not amount to thousands. The fate of Mr. Snider is a striking proof what estimate intellectual labour is held in. Some years ago a man discovered that certain poor iron ores in Scotland contained sufficient coal for their own smelting. The capitalists of the neighbourhood would not even advance the money to test the discovery by an experiment on a large scale, the man died in penury, and the capitalists are making fortunes out of his discovery at the present moment. This shews how capitalists value the intellectual acquirements of others—it is for the poor to value theirs. Let us look at the case from another side. According to Professor Leone Levi, the annual produce of the labour of the United Kingdom amounts to 745,000,000*l*. To raise this produce 10,697,000 people of both sexes, under sixty years of age are employed. They produce on an average 69*l*. a year and receive as remuneration 38*l*. a year. Now it is generally acknowledged as an axiom in political economy that labour determines the exchange value of goods, that is, that a certain quantity of labour embodied in a certain quantity of what will exchange for another certain quantity of labour embodied in the fourth edition of Mr. Mill's essay on political economy.

Thus, when the farmer buys books, and the publisher buys corn, real equivalents are exchanged between the so-called capitalist producer and the consumer. The case is different between the labouring producer and the capitalist appropriators. Out of every 69*l*. worth produced by the labouring class the capitalist class appropriates 31*l*. worth as a reward for having taken the trouble of appropriating a similar amount the previous year. This is the secret how one man can obtain 50,000*l*. out of a production that yields only 69*l*. per head of the effective labourers; it is the secret of the formation and accumulation of capital. The *Times'* correspondent at New York told us the other day that Alexander J. Stuart, merchant and importer of New York, had returned a taxable income for 1865 of 4,071,256 dollars, upon which he was to pay a tax of 407,000 dollars. Suppose Mr. Stuart to be an abstemious man, that he manages to defray his expenses with one half of his income, say *two million dollars,* that he devotes a hundred thousand a year to charitable purposes, and lays by 1,500,000 dollars. Without interest or profit upon these savings they would amount to 15,000,000 dollars in ten years; a pretty capital the result of abstinence.

Another case: A New York gentleman applied the other day to an insurance company whose policy he held for twenty-one thousand dollars to cover the loss of his daughter's wardrobe by fire. The young lady's wardrobe contained among other things twenty-six robes of silk and satin, two of velvet, twenty-four dresses of other stuffs, in all as many dresses as there are weeks in the year. There is not the remotest doubt that this young lady will some day bring to the man of her choice not only a rich store of clothing but also a considerable amount of capital— *the result of abstinence.* But whose abstinence? That of the Stuart's and the likes of that young lady—the abstinence of which Mr. Mill speaks? No; the plain, unsophisticated and untutored working men know far better—alas! from long and sad experience—what kind of parsimony and saving, and whose abstinence and compulsory privation lay the foundation for forming and accumulating capital.

That the working man receives only 2s. 5d. for every 4s. 7d. worth he produces is bad enough, but it is infinitely worse that out of this he has not only to pay his own share of local taxation but that of his landlord as well—in the house rent; he has to pay more than his share of the general taxation in the price of the articles he consumes, and, to add insult to injury, after all this, the whole host of sophists are continually telling him that he might save what he leads a dissipated life with.

III. Fundamental Propositions respecting Capital.

Sir W. Hamilton has stated that a man may think upon two subjects at the same time. Mr. Mill's capacities far exceed this. He can entertain two convictions upon the same subject, the one diametrically opposed to the other. He says: "While on the one hand industry is limited by capital, so on the other every increase of capital gives, or is capable of giving, additional employment to industry; and this without any assignable limit. ... Men of merit (Malthus, Dr. Chalmers, M. de Sismondi) have contended, that if consumers were to save and convert into capital more than a limited portion of their income, and were not to devote to unproductive consumption an amount of means bearing a certain ratio to the capital of the country, the extra accumulation would be so much waste, since there would be no market for the commodities which the capital so created would produce." To prove the contrary Mr. Mill continues: "Every one can see that if a benevolent government possessed all the food, and all the implements and materials, of the community, it could exact productive labour from all to whom it allowed a share in the food, and could be in no danger of wanting a field for the employment of this productive labour, since as long as there was a single want unsatisfied (which material objects could supply) of any one individual, the labour of the community could be turned to the production of something capable of satisfying that want. Now, the individual possessors of capital, when they add to it by fresh accumulations are doing precisely the same thing. Let us imagine the most extreme case conceivable. Suppose that every capitalist came to be of opinion that, not being more meritorious than a well conducted labourer, he ought not to fare better, and accordingly laid by, from conscientious motives, the surplus of his profits; or suppose this abstinence not spontaneous but imposed by law or opinion upon all capitalists and landowners likewise. ... The whole of what was previously expended in luxuries, by capitalists and landowners, is distributed among the existing labourers, in the form of additional wages. ... The increased accumulation and increased production might, rigorously speaking, continue, until every labourer had every indulgence of wealth consistent with continuing to work, supposing that the power of their labour were sufficient to produce all this amount of indulgences for the whole number. Thus the limit of wealth is never deficiency of consumers, but of producers."

Now for the contrary statements and admissions: "Dearth, or scarcity, on the one hand, and oversupply or, in mercantile language, glut on the other, are incident to all commodities. In the first case, the commodity affords to the producers or sellers, while the deficiency lasts, an unusually high profit; in the second, the supply being in excess of that for which a demand exists at such a value as will afford the ordinary rate of profit, the sellers must be content with less, and must even, in extreme cases, submit to a loss."

"If the present annual amount of savings were to continue without any of those counteracting circumstances which now keep in check the natural influence of those savings in reducing profits, the rate of profit would speedily attain the minimum, and all further accumulation of capital would for the present cease."

"The resisting agencies are of several kinds. First, is the waste of capital in periods of overtrading and rash speculation, and in the commercial revulsions by which such times are always followed. ... Mines are opened, railways or bridges made, and many other works of uncertain profit commenced, and in these enterprises much capital is sunk which yields either no return, or none adequate to the outlay. Factories are built and machinery erected beyond what the market requires or can keep in employment. ... Besides this there is a great unproductive consumption of capital during the stagnation which follows a period of general overtrading. Establishments are shut up or kept working without any profit, hands are discharged and numbers of persons in all ranks, being deprived of their income, and thrown for support on their savings, find themselves, after the crisis has passed away, in a condition of more or less impoverishment. By the time a few years have passed over without a crisis, so much additional capital has been accumulated, that it is no longer possible to invest it at the accustomed profit: all public securities rise to a high price, the rate of interest on the best mercantile securities falls very low, and the complaint is general among persons in business that no money is to be made. Does not this demonstrate how speedily profit would be at a minimum, and the stationary condition of capital would be attained, if these accumulations went on without any counteracting principle?"

Which is Napoleon and which is Wellington? Whichever you like, my little dear; take your choice. *The increase of capital gives employment without any assignable limits, overproduction is nonsense,* but, *the accumulation of capital would come to a standstill if overtrading did not periodically annihilate a large amount of capital, destroy implements of production, and throw hundreds of thousands out of work.*

And what is "overtrading" but over-production? Suppose that Mr. Stuart, at New York, imported 500,000*l.* worth of British hardwares five years ago and that his demand increased at the rate of ten per cent, per annum on the original amount, production would accommodate itself to the demand. But in the fifth year, his customers being well supplied, would principally replace the wear and tear of their old stock, and require only 400,000*l.* worth. The moment Mr. Stuart became aware of such a state of things he would telegraph to his agents here that he required no more at present; there would be £350,000 worth of unsaleable stock, and those who had bills discounted upon such stock might find their names in the *Gazette;* bankers would follow, workpeople would be put on short time, or factories shut up; other trades, having run in the same path, would follow the same course. There would be more means than ever of satisfying wants, but the mass of the people would starve and perish from want, because they could not pay for what they had produced *too much.* This is what is implied in the phrase "overtrading;" yet Mr. Mill asserts that there is no such thing as a general over-supply, above the demand, as far as it consists in the means of payment. *The reduction of profits to a minimum is the wind-up of the capitalist mode of production, the end of the contest between labour and capital, the emancipation of the hard-working, hard living, down-trodden millions.*

Although Mr. Mill refutes his own statements, his first supposition is, nevertheless, abstractedly true; but both the first and the second are totally incompatible with, and inapplicable to, the present state of society. The conception, it appears to me, stands in the same relation to the conception of the reality of such a state of things as the flying fish to the eagle. Mr. Mill has a faint anticipation of a state of things in which the satisfying of wants, and that alone, might be the incentive to production, but he cannot elevate his conception above a state of society in which the materials and instruments of production are the private property of individuals. As long as the prerequisites of production are the property of capitalists, so long will money-making continue to be the direct aim of production, so long will they abhor the idea "of not being more meritorious than a well-conducted labourer." As long as they obtain profits, so long the producers will have to work for wages, for less than their labour is worth, which will prevent "what was previously expended in luxuries to be distributed among them," and will preclude them from the indulgence of wealth; finally, as long as the capitalists are the controllers of production, so long no law or opinion will be imposed which will prevent those who work the least to get the most.

Now for the "benevolent Government." This supposition implies a state of society in which the materials and instruments of production are the joint property of the community, and the direction of production the function of the Government. It implies a state of society in which the old proverb "he who does not work neither shall he eat" has become a reality. It implies a state of society which has been preceded by such a course of training and education as the Congress of the International Workingmen's Association recommends for society at large; a state of society in which, if a thousand days' work is to be done, and a thousand men to do it, each will work a day. It implies a state of society in which the public Government performs the same functions as the directors of a joint-stock company for such a company. It implies a state of society of which the present co-operative movement is only the germ. There would not even be the semblance of benevolence about such a Government, it would only perform a bounden duty. As long as the members of a government are only the nominees of a class, so long they will have to legislate for, and defend, that class, and if that class happens to be in possession of all the materials and instruments of production, no amount of individual benevolence will enable the Government to direct production to the supplying of wants, instead of profit-making for individual proprietors.

IV. Excess of Supply.

Lest my readers should run away with the idea that Mr. Mill contradicts himself in the same breath, it is necessary to state that there is a considerable interval between the two statements I cited in my last article. The first, the hopeful view, which gives to the capitalist mode of production so universally beneficent a character, appears in the first volume, published in 1857; the second, the dry statement of the stern reality, occurs towards the end of the second volume, published in 1859. But between these statements there are others of a similar nature which require elucidation.

Recurring to the opinion of Malthus, Dr. Chalmers, and Sismondi, about overproduction, Mr. Mill says:—"When these writers speak of the supply of commodities as out-running the demand, it is not perfectly clear which of the two elements of demand they have in view—the desire to possess or the means to purchase; whether their meaning is that there are, in such cases, more consumable products in existence than the public desires to consume, or merely more than it is able to pay for. Let us suppose that the quantity of commodities produced is not greater than the community would be glad to consume: is it, in that case, possible that there should be a deficiency of demand for all commodities, for want of the means of payment? Those who think so cannot have considered what it is that constituted the means of payment for commodities. Each person's means of paying for the productions of other people consists of those which he himself possesses. All sellers are inevitably and *ex vi termini* buyers. Could we suddenly double the productive powers of the country, we should double the supply of commodities in every market; but we should, by the same stroke, double the purchasing power. Everybody would bring a double demand as well as a double supply: everybody would be able to buy twice as much in exchange. At any rate it is sheer absurdity that all things should fall in value, and that all producers should in consequence be insufficiently remunerated. If values remain the same, what becomes of prices is immaterial, since the remuneration of producers does not depend on how much money, but on how much of consumable articles, they obtain for their goods.

A general oversupply, or excess of all commodities above the demand, so far as demand consists in the means of payment is thus shown to be an impossibility."

Four chapters further we are told—"There is no absurdity in the hypothesis that of some given commodity a certain quantity is all that is wanted at any price."

Under existing circumstances I consider wheat as *the commodity* of which only a certain quantity is wanted at any price, and it is because wheat is an indispensable necessary of life, a commodity of which everybody, except those who are out of work, and those who are on the road to the workhouse, gets his share. What is the effect of the supply on the price of wheat? The following passage is quoted from Tooke's history of prices by Mr. Mill: —"The price of corn in this country has risen from 100 to 200 per cent. and upwards, when the utmost computed deficiency of the crops has not been more than between one sixth and one third below an average, and that deficiency relieved by foreign supplies." On the other hand when the supply exceeds the average the fall is as disproportionate. The agricultural statistics of France show that in 1817 the forty-eight millions of hectolitres of wheat harvested in that year were worth two thousand million francs, while nearly sixty-four millions, harvested in 1819, were only worth one thousand and one hundred millions. The increase of the produce was in the proportion of 3 to 4; the decrease in price was from 41 to 17 per hectolitre.

In this country the average price of wheat from 1850 to 1864 was about 2*l*. 10s. a quarter. The average price for the year 1851 was 38s. 6d. a quarter with a supply of home, and foreign wheat of 42,391,875 cwts.; in 1855 the supply fell to 36,469,782 cwts., and the price for the year rose to 74s. 8d. For every seven 41b. loaves that had been baked in 1851 there were but six in 1855, but the six cost nearly six shillings, while the seven were sold for something like three shillings and sixpence. The cause of these fluctuations is this: whether bread is dear or cheap the poor must have a certain quantity to support life; if bread be dear all other articles of consumption have to be curtailed, some even abandoned, to obtain bread. There is even a possibility of more bread being consumed in the poorest families when it is sufficiently dear to prevent the consumption of butcher's meat. There is little difference in the quantity of wheat consumed whether it is dear or cheap unless it reaches the famine price. When the price of bread falls, the poor, instead of eating more bread, increase their consumption of everything else that comes within their reach, except bread. This explains the reason why butcher's meat rises in price when bread is cheap, and remains stationary when bread is dear.

Next to wheat, butcher's meat is an article the consumption of which could not be increased beyond the actual want. The well-to-do getting already as much as they require, no fall in the price would induce them to eat more. A fall in the price, or an increase in the means of payment of the poor would no doubt result in a large increase in the consumption of butcher's meat; but, like bread, it would have its limit. What holds good with bread and meat holds good with every other article of commerce, with this difference, that the means of payment and the desire to possess, of those who have the means, are the limits of the demand. The rich could buy more gold watches than they do, but they buy only a certain number, and if the watch makers make more than the rich are willing to buy, the surplus is overproduction that cannot be sold at all, or must be sold at a loss to people who are either not willing or not able to buy at the remunerative price. The gentlemen who wear the broad cloth, which the London drapers cannot sell for less than 25s. a yard, require only a certain quantity, if much more were produced it would be dead stock.

Now, we are ready to enter upon the examination of Mr. Mill's supposition. Suppose the Wizard of the North could by one stroke double the production of everything, except man himself, his stomach and his stature, two suits of clothes, two quarters of wheat, two cwts. of beef, and two ounces of gold would respectively represent the same amount of labour as before, and ought to exchange in the same proportion as they do now, otherwise it would not be *immaterial what became of prices.*

Under existing circumstances the selling price is the form in which the labour exchange value must be realised. Amongst the various products of labour gold is the only one of which everybody is ready to appropriate any conceivable amount. Everything else is produced to be sold for gold; it is only with respect to the commodity gold that *all sellers are inevitably buyers,* hence it is that the quantity of gold which a given article will realise, determines the success or failure of the producer, and what becomes of prices is of the utmost consequence.

Suppose our old friend, farmer Brown, came to market with twice as much wheat as he used to, and the forestalled the miller, and the baker, had twice as much gold as they used to have; but, having lately discovered that the poor, instead of eating more bread on account of it being more abundant, were drinking more beer, eating more meat, and looking out for finer clothes than formerly, they would only buy the customary quantity of wheat, its price would, at the very least, fall from 40s. to 20s., and farmer Brown's purchasing power, instead of having doubled would be reduced by 50 per cent., while the liabilities—liabilities which could only be met by hard cash—

would have increased 100 per cent. Suppose the farmer was in a position to tide over the difficulty for a season, would he continue working his farm as before? Certainly not. He would employ fewer hands, buy fewer implements, none at all for a season, land would be thrown out of cultivation and rents would fall, and the purchasing power of the farmer's tradesmen and their workpeople would be reduced to zero. We see now that it matters very materially *what becomes of prices* and that Mr. Mill's supposition about everybody's purchasing power being doubled is sheer nonsense.

I have selected wheat to illustrate the subject, because it exhibits the phenomena to which I desired to direct the reader's attention, in the most striking and unmistakable manner. That many other commodities would, at the very outset, share the fate of wheat is beyond question, particularly mere necessaries. There are some which are both necessaries and luxuries, the consumption of which is not limited by want. Upon an increase of means, the poor might far more than double their use of furniture and clothing, either by a direct increase, or by replacing old ones by new and better, without being extravagant. Although a man could not eat a dozen times as much as another decently fed man, there are plenty [of] vain people, fond of show, who wear out, or spoil, a dozen suits of clothes where other decently dressed folks will make one suit suffice. In the same way a man may keep a number of carriages and horses to match; but no one will keep two carts and horses for the work that one can do. The dead lock to production will therefore arrive sooner with regard to necessaries than luxuries. On the other hand what tends most to a greater steadiness in the prices of manufactured goods than of wheat is, that production can be arrested at any stage of the process when prices decline, and that it can be accelerated when they rise, and that few are so hard pressed as not to be able to suspend purchasing for a time when prices run too high. Nevertheless a general over supply and a ruinous fall of prices periodically occur, as Mr. Mill so distinctly points out.

V. Effect of the Demand for Commodities on the Demand for Labour.

On this subject we have a statement, a contradiction, and a prevarication. If a simpleton were asked why so many geese are brought to London at Christmas time, he would probably reply—why, because the people want them for Christmas dinner, you know. There is also a notion abroad that country people rear and fatten geese for the very purpose of selling them to the London dealers, and that the London dealers bring them to market because they know, from experience, that many people would not be contented without a Christmas goose. But this is an every day view of the matter. Mr. Mill endeavours to dispute the correctness of this vulgar notion. He says: —"What supports and employs productive labour is the capital expended setting it to work, and not the demand of purchasers for the produce of the labour when completed. Demand for commodities is not demand for labour." According to this version it is not the knowledge of the fact that the London people buy so many geese that induces country people to rear many more than they want for themselves, but it is because they are fond of, and have the means for, rearing geese that they do it. What does the following passage, in the *Times* of November 19, imply?—"The manufacturers' order books are very badly supplied—insufficiently in many instances to keep the men working nearly full time." This is from Birmingham. Are orders a "demand for the produce of labour when completed" or not? Do these orders exercise any influence upon the amount of labour employed by the hardware manufacturer or not? But independent of the fact, that the employment of a very considerable amount of labour, in many branches of industry, depends upon the direct orders and demand of the consumers for finished goods, what is the ruling guide for the employment of labour, in those branches of industry' in which the production of ready made goods is the rule, and orders the exception? The facility to sell. The trade reports of November 17 are: Bradford, "Stocks increase and prices droop. Manufacturers of plain goods are working short time." Leeds, "Several large woollen mills are working short time." Manchester, "The manufacturers in the surrounding districts have unanimously resolved to work four days a week instead of six; in many other parts of Lancashire spindles and looms by thousands are idle." "In making sales of either yarn or cloth the manufacturers have almost to force them on the market at a heavy reduction." I ask, then, does the demand for commodities determine the demand for labour or not? Is it from want of capital, or is it from want of purchasers that the factory labourers are put on short time?

Let us now hear what Mr. Mill has to say in elucidating his erroneous statement. He continues: —"Suppose, for instance, that there is a demand for velvet; a fund ready to be laid out in buying velvet but no capital to establish the manufacture. It is of no consequence how great the demand may be; unless capital is attracted into the occupation, there will be no velvet made, and consequently none bought, unless the intending purchaser makes advances to workpeople that they may make velvet, *i.e.,* to convert part of his own income into capital. Let us now reverse the hypothesis, and suppose that there is plenty of capital ready for making velvet but no demand, velvet will not be made.

Manufacturers and their labourers do not produce for the pleasure of their customers, but for the supply of their own wants, and having still the capital and the labour, which are the essentials of production, they can either produce something which is in demand, or if there be no demand, they themselves have one, and can produce things which they want for their own consumption."

This is "confusion worse confounded," and logic most unmercifully outraged. Let us analyse this kettle of fish. If velvet can be made after an advance of money by the intending purchaser, then the prerequisites to the production of velvet, Mr. Mill's capital *per se,* must exist in a latent state, waiting to be absorbed in the process of velvet making. But Mr. Mill does not dispute this. He has for the moment forgotten the caution he gave at the outset, he confounds money with capital; what he really means to say is, that though there may be workmen possessing the requisite knowledge and skill for making velvet, the tools and materials in the warehouse of the dealer ready to enter the workshop upon their price being tendered, and the purchasing price of the velvet in the hands of the intending purchaser, if no intermeddler, possessing a third equivalent in money, step in to purchase the tools and materials and employ the workpeople velvet will not be made, unless the intending purchaser and the workmen contrive to do without him. Mr. Mill tells us that in this case, the intending purchaser converts part of his income into capital. No such thing. What he advances is, the whole or part of the price of the velvet, which he parts with to gratify a desire. In gratifying this desire he may also satisfy a want, that of clothing himself; but he expects no pecuniary return—nothing beyond the pleasure of wearing velvet and displaying his wealth. His advancing money to obtain velvet is no more an investment of capital than a gentleman advancing money to an ostler to procure him a fine horse for his carriage. The money invested in the purchase of Pickford's vans and horses and the wages paid to the drivers, form an outlay which is expected to replace itself with a profit, hence it is capital; but the money expended for the horses and carriages of the Marquis of Westminster, and the wages paid to his grooms and coachmen form no outlay, it is expenditure which is not expected to yield anything beyond the pleasure which horses and carriages afford, hence it is not capital. The simple admission that velvet can be made without the capitalist employer, if the demand for it be accompanied by its purchasing price, is fatal to Mr. Mill's fundamental proposition. According to the ordinary rules of reasoning the reversed hypothesis should, at least, hide the wound which this side stab has inflicted, but, instead of doing that, it enlarges it into an irreparable rent, for it states positively that with all the capital in the world being ready for velvet making, if there be no demand, velvet will not be made. We are thus irresistibly led to the conclusion that if the demand for a commodity be accompanied by its purchasing price the commodity will be produced, but that in the known absence of a demand nothing will be produced; hence demand for goods, and not capital as such, creates the demand for labour.

Mr. Mill is fully conscious of this, but his unbounded faith in the inherent propensities of capital to promote production at all hazards leads him to have recourse to prevarication. How do people supply their own wants in modern society? By making, from the cradle to the grave, things for everybody's use except their own. The cotton-miller and his hands, the tailors, the shoemakers, etc., do not enter into business to be able to make cotton, cloth, clothes, shoes, for themselves, but that by making these things for the pleasure of their customers they may get cotton, clothes, shoes, bread, meat, etc., for themselves. If their customers desire nothing they get nothing themselves. Mr. Mill says: —"Having the labour and the capital if there be no demand for one thing they can make another." Can they? The velvet-makers have been engaged in velvet making from their very childhood. All that has fallen to their share in the shape of consumables they got for velvet making, but they never wore any themselves. The demand stops. The ladies have taken it into their heads to wear cashmere shawls instead of velvet cloaks. What is to be done? Transfer the capital will be the ready reply of political economists. But the capital, in as far as it consists in tools and materials, is not transferable to the making of the article for which there is a demand nor the acquired skill of the labourer. The only thing transferable is the ready money that may be in the possession of their employers, but with this they assuredly will not employ their former hands, the velvet makers, and the only possible way in which the latter can produce anything to supply their own wants is by making velvet for the pleasure of other people. In the case of there being no demand for anything, capitalists and labourers setting to work to produce things for their own consumption, this is such a preposterous supposition that one can hardly take it as serious. The idea of the cotton millers of Lancashire giving their capital that their spinners and weavers might produce food, shelter, shoes, even cotton shirts for themselves. Did the capitalists of Lancashire invest a single five pound note by way of business with such an end in view during the late crisis? If half the population of London were going naked from want of clothes, not a yard of cloth would be produced to cover their nakedness by way of business, unless there was a well founded belief that those who furnished it would be paid for it. Capital never employs labour with a view of satisfying wants or desires, unless those who have the want or the desire are also willing and able to give the capitalist more for the finished product than he gives to his work-people. Whatever capitalist acts contrary to this, renders himself liable to loss, insolvency, and ruin.

VI. Fixed Capital—Its Effect upon Labour.

All contrivances that are got up with a view to aid or promote production, and are not rendered useless by being used once, come under the head of fixed capital. It is not my intention to treat of fixed capital generally, but only of those contrivances which are generally termed "improvements of production," and which enter into immediate competition with living labour.

Mr. Mill supposes the case of a farmer who employs 2,000 qrs. of corn per annum in maintaining labourers producing 2,400 qrs., altering his mind, and one year expending 1,000 qrs. for the improvement of land, half the labourers would be thrown out of employment at the end of the year. He says: —"This improvement may, with the diminished quantity of labour, produce as much corn as before. This will enable the farmer to become a larger employer of labour. But the improvement may only produce 1,500 qrs., this will be a gain of 25 per cent., on the whole capital instead of 20 per cent., but permanent injury to labourers." That an improvement in production, which brings grist to the mill of the capitalist, should only bring starvation to the labourer, is rather a bold supposition and Mr. Mill amends it by saying, "Nevertheless, I do not believe that as things are actually transacted, improvements in production are often, if ever, injurious, even temporarily, to the labouring classes in the aggregate."

This is simply a skuffle. What consolation is it to the poor wight whose labour has been rendered useless by, no matter what, improvement that others get the article he used to produce a trifle cheaper if the improvement has had the effect of depriving him of the means of subsistence? But the injury does not stop here. If the labour of one half is rendered useless that of the other half becomes depreciated, and a depreciation in any one branch generally, and immediately, affects all kindred branches; but an improvement in the direction of the latter portion of Mr. Mill's supposition would not only have the effect of depreciating labour, it would, by diminishing the produce also enhance its price, and the farmer's gain would be everybody else's loss. But why have recourse to hypothetical suppositions at all? Are there no real, heart-stirring—aye, and heart-rending facts, to illustrate the subjects? Facts that admit no equivocating beliefs? Is it not a fact that in consequence of the improvement in agriculture the number of labourers is as steadily diminishing as the produce is increasing? Is the increase in the wages of labour more than, or even equal to the depreciation of gold since 1851?

Facts are said to be stubborn things. I have before me a pamphlet—"Stubborn facts from the factories, by a Manchester Operative." John Ollivier, Pall Mall, London, 1844, from which I will give a few extracts.

The raw cotton consumed in this country amounted in 1781 to 5,198,778lbs; in 1841 it amounted to 528,000,000lbs; in 1781 the hand loom weaver obtained 33s. 3d., for weaving 20 yards; in 1841, 3s. 9d. for weaving 24 yards. The power loom weavers of Sidebottom's mill, Waterside, received in 1823, for weaving 24 yards, 21 picks to the quarter inch, 2s.; in 1841, one more pick to the quarter 1s. Ashton's Mill, Newton Moor, 1825, for 24 yards, 2s. 8d.; 1836, ditto, 1s. 2d.

The spinners received in 1806, for one thousand hanks, forty hanks to the pound, 9s. 2d.; in 1823, 6s. 3d.; in 1832, 3s. 8d.; and in 1843, from 1s. l0d. to 2s. 3d.; and one shilling only where self-acting mules were employed. In Houldsworth's fine mill, there were in 1829, 127 spinners and 83,376 spindles; Thirty-five of the largest firms employed in 1829 one thousand spinners, 674,074 spindles; in 1841 there were but 487 spinners working 736,128 spindles. Thirty-six coarse firms employed in 1829, 1,088 spinners; 1841 only 448, working 53,353 spindles more than the larger number in 1829. Between 1835 and 1843 the number of spinners employed

in Stockport dwindled down from 800 to 140. A fortunate who had remained in work, stated in 1843, "In 1840 I was working on wheels carrying 672 spindles, and could earn 1*l*. 2s. a week. I now work upon a pair of wheels carrying 2,040 spindles and earn 13s. a week." This is more than doubling the productive power.

The Fustian cutters were paid in 1827, 4d. a yard; 1843, 1 1/2 d. a yard; women and children employed.

In a petition to Parliament from the blockprinters of Lancashire, Cheshire, and Derbyshire, 1842, it is stated that 10,000,000 pieces were printed by machines, for which the printers and their boys would have received 1,125,000*l.*; the wages of those who attended these machines was 29,000*l.*, and with this improvement in production children from 7 to 9 years old had to work from 16 to 18 hours a day.

Perhaps some of my readers may be led to the conclusion that the machine makers must have had a jolly time of it, let us see; I give in full what is said on this subject: —"Introduced between the year 1838 and 1844 in one of the large machine making shops of Manchester:

One plaining machine, equal to fourteen men employs one man or boy to direct it. Five smaller ones equal to three men each, employ one person each.

One blotting machine equal to twelve men, one person directs it.

One self-acting lathe equal to three men, with one person to superintend it.

One nut-cutting machine equal to three men, employs one boy.

One wheel-cutting machine, equal to twenty men, employs one man.

One boring machine, equal to ten men, employs one person.

In another shop there are twenty self-acting lathes, equal to one hundred men, one man or a boy attends two of them.

Eight plaining machines, equal to ninety-six men, one man or a boy attends one of them.

One nut-cutting, upon a further improved principle, equal to twenty men, employs one boy only.

One slotting machine, equal to twenty men, one man or boy to direct it."

Hardly a day passes without some political wiseacre talking about the benefits conferred upon the working-classes by a rapid increase in the accumulation of capital, but here we see that in the very branch of industry, the name of which is synonymous with all that is modern in production—all that is typical of the capitalist mode—the accumulation of capital has had no other effect, during a space of fifty years, than that of displacing labour, and depreciating what was not displaced. The man, the husband, the father, the natural protector and provider of the family was sent home from the factory to cook and mend stockings, and the wife and the little children had to take his place in the mill to procure him food.

Beliefs do not easily go down with everybody now-a-days, and it requires a very credulous person indeed to believe that improvements in *production are not even temporarily injurious to the labouring classes.* Did the hand loom weavers of 1841 stick to their trade from choice? What became of those who were turned adrift? The author says: —"Great numbers may be seen about the streets selling salt; gathering rags and bones; sweeping the streets; anything that may offer the least apology for a livelihood."

Thus the capitalist mode of production is at best a social war *in permanence,* improvement of the productive power going about like a roaring lion seeking whom it can devour; it is a cruel war, all the victory and the shooting is on one side, and the being shot at on the other; it is a detestable, abominable war, engendered by greed—undisguised greed—rendered the more hateful because the accumulation of wealth, for the sake of accumulation, is held up as an ennobling principle, is looked upon by its votaries as a divine ordinance, or a natural law, and is represented as humane and beneficial in its effects upon the poor by apologetic sophists and mountebanks. Those who perish in the struggle have not even the consolation of falling in a good cause or dying for glory, they are void of all fanaticism, of illusion, and delusion; they are simply victims sacrificed at the shrine of Plutus; they are conscious of their doom, and see themselves perish inch by inch.

VII. The Cost of Production.

This is one of the burning questions upon which the two main divisions of the population, that constitute modern society, will never come to an agreement. Those who are in possession of all the food, the clothing, the shelter, and the implements and materials of production, consider the question from a utilitarian, those who possess nothing but the requisite ingenuity, skill, dexterity, and muscular strength for manual operations, from a humanitarian point of view. A reconciliation of these stand-points is utterly impossible, and conversion is out of the question. A writer in the *Daily Telegraph* said the other day that, if such men as George Odger were sent into the House of Commons, their erroneous notions on questions of political economy would melt like wax before the fire, before the eloquence of Mr. Gladstone. Vain delusion! This is only the conversion of time servers and place hunters. It is not a matter of comprehension but of social position. It is hardly probable, if it were possible, that the cottier, who is under notice to quit, to make room for sheep, because wool and mutton are dear; and the spinner, whose employer is about to invest his previous year's income, which the spinner has helped to produce, in self-acting machinery to supersede manual labour, should be equally convinced of the advantages of the change with the landlord and the millowner. The representative spokesman of an aspiring class, or an advanced party, are inconvertible. From the moment they exhibit signs of softening they cease to be representative leaders. Had Richard Cobden and John Bright softened before the charms of protectionist eloquence they would no longer have been the spokesmen of the industrial middle-class, and would certainly have been repudiated as turn coats and deserters. Others would have taken their places.

In a rational state of society the cost of production of the annual produce of the community would be equal to the amount of labour required to produce it. But under existing arrangements this is not the case. The utilitarians, the owners of all the produce of labour, call that portion of the produce which they have to expend to obtain the whole, the cost of production.

If a farmer required twenty horses for the ploughing of his land, whatever quantity of grain and hay they consumed would be reckoned as cost of production, and he would consider his horses very useful as long as he could not do without them. But if, by some mechanical contrivance, the ploughs were so much improved that they could be worked with half the horse-power, ten horses would become useless; if, by a further improvement, the ploughs could be worked by a ten-horse power steam engine, at half the expense of the keep of the ten living horses, all the horses would become useless. These improvements might tend to a large increase of the produce of the farm, larger than what would be required to feed all the horses as before, yet if the farmer could not sell them all, and was not allowed to kill them or turn them adrift, he would consider himself injured if he had to provide food for any one of them until it died a natural death, though the work of these very horses might in the first instance have furnished the means to purchase the improved machinery. This is precisely the utilitarian, the bourgeois point of view. The proprietors of all the wealth are, as it were, morally convinced that they have an indisputable right to it, and consider every farthing of expense, besides what they spend for their own enjoyment, as a waste and an injury unless it be used or used up in the production and increase of their wealth. In the actual state of things the cost of production consists of the quantity of the produce of labour that is necessary to keep a certain number of productive agents in working condition, and replacing them when they are worn out. There is no difference between the steam engine, the horse, and the man. The engine requires fuel and water; the horse, grain, hay, and water; the man, bread, meat, and drink, to keep them in working condition; all else is luxury. Mr. Mill says, "as much of the wages of labour as exceeds the actual necessaries of life and health is not actually applied to production, but to the unproductive consumption of productive labourers, indicating a fund for production sufficiently ample to admit of habitually diverting a part of it to a mere convenience."

Nor is there any difference between the horse and the man respecting the danger of becoming useless.

Dr. Ure, one of the greatest panegyrists of the factory system says:—"The constant aim and tendency of every improvement in machinery is to supersede human labour altogether, or to diminish its cost, by substituting the industry of women and children for that of men; or of ordinary labourers for trained artizans. On the automatic plan, skilled labour gets progressively superseded, and will eventually be replaced by mere overlookers of machines. Mr. Anthony Strutt, of Belper and Milford. will employ no man who has learned his craft; but in contempt of the division of labour principle, he sets a plough boy to turn a shaft of several tons weight, and never has reason to repent his preference. The effect of substituting the self-acting mule for the common mule, is to discharge the greater part of the men spinners, and to retain adolescents and children. The proprietor of a factory near Stockport states that by such substitution, he would save 50*l.* a week in wages, in consequence of dispensing with nearly forty male spinners." (This was written 30 years ago.)

However loud the millowner may sing on Sunday "No more than others I deserve but God has given me more," he would be exceedingly shocked if his workpeople told him point blank on Monday morning that they considered themselves entitled to a share in such improvements.

But there is a difference between those horses and men that have not yet become useless. As long as the horse is used the useless ones do not deprive him of his food, but the unemployed men deprive the employed ones of food by forcing their wages down below the point of subsistence. Remember the Stockport spinner cited in my last. There is another difference between the man and the horse, the man has a will of his own. Left to the bourgeois rule of supply and demand, and to cope single-handed with the capitalist, the labourer would be at the mercy of the employer. But, in combination with his fellow workmen he can exact somewhat better terms. The trades unions and factory laws are a bitter pill, a very bitter pill, for the spokesman of the capitalists to swallow, but there is no help. Thirty years ago Dr. Ure showed that in consequence of trades unions and factory laws the English millowners had to pay 11s. average wages for 69 hours work weekly, while in France the factory hands worked from 72 to 84 hours for 5s. 8d., and in Bonn in Prussia, 94 hours for 2s. 6d. A week ago, two men, who have visited the coal and iron works in Belgium, enlarged in the *Times* upon the happiness of the Belgian coal and iron masters who, owing to the absence of trades' unions and factory laws, can make the whole families of their operatives work more hours for less money than the puddlers in the black country obtain for their own individual labour.

However willing a portion of the aristocracy is to impose restrictions upon the mill-lords, they are quite as utilitarian in their own sphere as landlords. Not long ago a noble lord, who has rendered signal service to the factory labourers, endeavoured to prove that the rustic labourers in his county were well paid, that if they were good boys they could, by a series of shifts and problematical advantages make 14s. a week. The Bishop of Oxford, and one of his subordinates, consider the clergy, the nobility, and the gentry, above all blame, because a labourer in the neighbourhood of Windsor Castle, who has *eleven children,* has never earned less than twelve shillings a week and sometimes as much as fifteen. Because the agricultural labourers vegetate and rear children, and cultivate on an average 28 acres of land each, on twelve shillings a week, nobody, in the opinion of these noble lords, has any business to find fault. Lord Dufferin, an Irish landlord, thinks that as one labourer is enough in Great Britainfor every 28 acres of land, Ireland requires no more. According to his calculation there are still 300,000 out of 800,000 too many, *i.e.* according to the English system only 500,000 are necessary to do the work; the other 300,000 are useless and a burden upon the land, he advises them to emigrate.

Mr. Arnold, of Manchester, wishes to retain this surplus population, because he is quite sure that before long, as soon as raw cotton becomes cheap, some 40,000 hands will be required in the cotton mills. Forty thousand seems to be a sort [of] standard want. Dr. Ure calculated in 1836, that the steam power then in course of erection would require 45,000 hands. There was a great demand for children at that time. By an Act of Parliament, which took effect on the 1st of March, 1836, children under twelve years of age were prohibited from working longer than 48 hours a week in cotton mills. About 16,400 children under twelve years were rescued by this Act from the cotton mills. It was a severe blow at a time when the trade increased at an unparalleled rate, and when millions were invested in machinery to enable little children and plough-boys to supersede high paid and skilled workmen to lower the cost of production. However, the Government of the day took compassion upon the mill-owners, and appointed migration agents in the factory districts, who had to arrange terms with the employers for the pauper children which were sent from the rural districts to be employed in the mills. In a circular letter to the Clerks of the Boards of Guardians, dated Somerset House, 23rd October, 1835, it is stated "The families most eligible will be those of widows with the greatest number of grown up children. In cotton, wool, and flax mills, the manufacturers prefer children above twelve years of age, as not interrupting the continuous course of daily employment. In silk mills there is no restriction, and in such factories they are generally preferred at eight years and upwards." During the spring quarter about a hundred families migrated. Some were engaged for three years, others till they should complete their twentieth year. But trade getting sick this migration did not attain any large dimensions. The 45,000 hands were not required. The export of cotton goods, which had risen from 20,513,586*l.* in 1834, to 24,632,058*l.* in 1836, fell in 1837 to 20,596,123*l.*

This is the way in which the utilitarians, the chiefs of production and the proprietors of all the produce of labour manage to keep the cost of production low. Lord Dufferin is as consistent in endeavouring to rid Ireland of the useless labourers, as Mr. Arnold is in wishing to retain a surplus. The cost of the maintenance of the agricultural labourer is already so low that hardly a reduction is possible, and therefore a surplus is a real burden. It is not so with the factory workers. They still get a little more than will keep skin and bone together, and a surplus of hungry applicants for work, will in an emergency either enable the mill owner to make a reduction, or prevent those at work from demanding a rise.

VIII. The Cost of Production.

If Dr. Ure's ideal could be realised—if all the productive labour could be performed by automatic machines—the cost of production would be reduced to the cost of the materials required for the making of the machines; all social and political strife would be at an end, the rich would enjoy their wealth in peace. There being no longer any demand for human labour— the sole condition of existence of the labouring poor—the working population would be, more or less, gradually improved out of existence; none but the proprietors of wealth and their menials could subsist. If the improvement of the productive powers, the lowering of the cost of production, that has taken place in the manufacture of cotton could be extended to all branches of labour, fewer than a hundred thousand human beings would have to be maintained to produce the same amount of wealth as is now produced by ten millions of hired wages labourers. Such a result would be in strict accordance with our established laws and usages, and the inevitable result of the much-vaunted law of supply and demand.

The doctrine, that a thing is worth what it will fetch in the market, applied to labour simply means, that the value of the working man's life ought to be determined by the very same rules by which the value of the lives of horses, the existence or non-existence of horses and steam-engines, is determined.

Those who treat labour as a commodity cannot have the remotest idea that there is no analogy between what the working man has to dispose of and the commodity which the capitalist has to sell. What the capitalist has to sell is a finished product, totally dissevered from any personal consideration. As soon as he has pocketed the purchasing price, it does not concern him *when, where,* and *how* the thing sold is to be used. A man may buy a ship to convey it to the high sea for the purpose of setting it on fire to witness the grand spectacle of a burning ship, or he may use it for a voyage to the Arctic regions or to circumnavigate the globe—it does not concern the ship-builder; but it seriously concerns the working man *when, where,* and *how* his labour is to be used. The working man has nothing to sell. What he has to dispose of is not a product, a thing separate or separable from his own individual *self;* he hires out his capacity to perform certain manual operations, and in doing so he hires himself out, and, with certain provisoes, he hands his *own self* over to his employer for the whole space of time requisite to execute the labour contracted for. The only analogy there is in the actual state of things is, that both the commodity of the capitalist and the labourer become useless if no one has any need for it—that is, if it will not fetch a price in the market. This, to the working man, is tantamount to extinction.

If, as the utilitarians maintain, a man may do what he likes with his own, then, as long as the pre-requisites of production are private property, the proprietors have an indisputable right to substitute the steam-engine for the living horse and the automatic spinner and weaver for the living man spinner and weaver; and, if the mill-owner has the right to substitute the engine and the automaton for the horse and the man, every other proprietor has the right to follow the example; and, if the spinner and the weaver are in duty bound to submit and make their exit, then the whole labouring population would be in duty bound to submit and make their exit if their labour were no longer useful to the possessors of wealth. They might do this as cheerfully as the maniacs who throw themselves before the wheels of the Car of Juggernaut if they would only look upon the cost of production from the proprietary point of view, and learn to understand that the law of supply and demand is either an immutable law of nature or a Divine ordinance.

However, the possessors of wealth and their spokesmen cannot help being tickled now and then by a touch of humanitarian considerations, but they easily get over it by not believing that the improvement of the productive powers injures the labouring poor in the long run. Thomas Ashton stated before a Parliamentary committee in 1824: "There is at the present moment a gradual transfer of workmen going on from handlooms to powerlooms; this transfer of hands, by enabling me to perform the same quantity of work with much fewer hands, does not throw many workmen out of work. Our trade is advancing in such a rapid degree as to absorb the number of hands thus thrown out. The men earn from twenty-four to thirty shillings a week clear money for dressing. The weaving is done by boys and women." Besides the

fact that it would have required a sixfold increase of weaving to place the superseded handloom weavers, a dressing machine was soon invented by which one boy could do the work of four men. Professor Venior—no champion of labour's rights-said in 1830: "Ever since the introduction of the powerloom, thousands of hand-loom weavers have been pining away under misery not alleviated even by hope." Mr. Cowell, a factory inspector, gave an account of an improvement of two mills in Manchester. The mules, containing 324 spindles, and spinning 16lbs. of cotton (200 hanks to the pound) in 69 hours, had been doubled. One man worked 648 spindles, spinning 32lbs. earning 50s. instead of 41s. as before. Mr. Cowell forgot that the extra nine shillings necessarily deprived another man of 41s., and that it could only last until the improvement became general.

At that very time Messrs. Sharp and Roberts stated, among the advantages of using their self-actors, "the saving of a spinner's wages to each pair of mules, and increased production." The 648 spindle mule was soon thrown in the shade. In 1835, Dr. Ure wrote: "It is delightful to see from 800 to 1,000 spindles of polished steel advancing and receding. One spinner manages a pair, and supersedes the labour of one or two companions." To his own query whether this will not effect a reduction of wages he has no other answer but that he is certain it increases the wages of children, makes the spinners civil and obedient, and gives the millowner a chance of selecting the best.

"The men displaced might find employment upon the power-looms at 15s. a week." Thus we see that the value of a powerloom situation had diminished by half in the short space of ten years. Inspector Horner reported in Oct. 1843, "hundreds of men between twenty and thirty years of age, in full vigour, are employed as piecers at 8s. or 9s. a week, while children of thirteen receive 5s., and young women between sixteen and twenty from 10s. to 12s." There are none so blind and deaf as those who will neither see nor hear. G.R.Porter, the late secretary of the Board of Trade, says in his Progress of the Nation, 1851: "Piecers are employed in the proportion of four to one spinner; one is generally a girl. The progress of trade is so gigantic that the boys are all absorbed as spinners; they increase in a geometrical ratio." This statement proves that such glowing accounts should, at all times, be received with great caution, if not with distrust.

I shall now give a few facts to show what the nineteenth century has accomplished in the shape of reducing the cost of production and increasing the productive powers. Dr. Ure calculates that at the very least a Hindoo woman would have to work 500 days to spin a pound of cotton into 250 hanks; according to a statement in a little book published by the Society for the Diffusion of Useful Knowledge, one horse-power could spin as much as 1,066 persons, proving the tendency of modern civilisation to replace 1,066 human beings by a horse. Hargreaves' Jenny enabled one person to spin from 16 to 20 threads at one time; Highs' increased it to more than 50; Arkwright's to 100, and introduced horse-power to turn the machine. Crompton invented the mule, a hybrid between the Jenny and the water-frame with 130 spindles; this, as I have already mentioned, was improved to a thousand. Next came the reduction of friction and accelerated motion. The Throstle required one horse-power for 180 spindles, the mule one for 500 spindles. Gore's spindles turned 5,000 in the minute; Axton's 7,000 times. In 1823 one spinner with 336 spindles could turn off 46lbs., 120 hanks to the pound, in 74 1/2 hours per week; in

1833, the same number of spindles 52 1/2 lbs. in 69 a week. In 1829 the spinner turned off 312 pounds of yarn in the same time that he turned off 648 in 1835. The cotton wool consumed in 1801 amounted to 56,000,000lbs., in 1859 to 973,800,000 pounds. The cotton consumed per horse-power was 6,309lbs. in 1839; in 1856 it was 8,670 pounds. The cotton consumed per spindle in 1812, 15lbs.; 1856, 30lbs.

Kay's fly shuttle, doubling the weaving power, was introduced 1738. About the time of the introduction of the power loom a good handloom weaver could weave two pieces of 24 yards each, in a week. In 1823 a girl or boy fifteen years old attending two power looms, could weave seven pieces of equal length; in 1826 from 12 to 15 pieces. The number of power looms at work in the cotton trade in Great Britain were:

1820	1829	1833
14,150	55,500	100,000.

In the United Kingdom 1835, 109,626; in 1856, 299,000. Cotton cloth exported per loom 1835, 5,100 yards; 1856, 6,800 yards. To spin the cotton consumed in 1859 on the old household wheel would require more than 60,000,000 persons; half a million men, women, and children, perform all the labour required. In 1811 there were 35 out of every hundred engaged in agriculture; in 1841 but 22. The total number of agricultural labourers in 1841 was 1,499,278; in 1851, 1,347,387; in 1861, 1,340,000. The value of the mining produce was 9,000,000*l.* in 1812. In 1858 it amounted to 31,266,932*l.* In 1795 the export of our produce and manufactures was 27,312,338*l.*; in 1865 it was 165,862,402*l.* The export of British goods amounted to 27,312,338*l.*; in 1865 to 165,862,402*l.* In 1842 the income charged with income tax amounted to 203,619,116*l.*; in 1864 to 303,652,868*l.* That this development of the productive powers, and the consequent increase of wealth, borders on the marvellous, none but a madman will deny; that with such productive powers at command it is a scandal to civilization that the hardest working population that ever existed, or any portion of them should even be exposed to the possibility of suffering privations, much less going actually short of food, not even a Ure can have the hardihood to contradict. The working man maintains that he has a natural right to live whether his existence increases the wealth of the rich or not; he is, moreover, morally convinced that all the improvements of the productive powers ought to be, and at no very distant date will be, the common inheritance of the human species instead of a source of extermination to some of the most valuable sections. These improvements belong to no class, no age, no country; the man who made the first wheel has as great a share in the most improved machine, that will be in the forthcoming Paris exhibition, as the maker of it. Had he not found the wheel and other contrivances ready for use he would have had to invent them before he could go any further.

IX. Credit.

Before I proceed with the present subject, I must apologise for the blunders in my last. Those who have experienced the pleasure of carrying on literary pursuits at the family fireside, amidst the prattle of the non-literary members, will probably make some allowance. The professor's name I quoted is not "Venior," but Senior, the celebrated opponent of factory legislation who taught political economy at Oxford, at the time when some of our present experienced legislators were young hopefuls at college. The spirit of his teachings may be gathered from the following specimen which occurs in the preface to lectures on the wages question delivered in 1830: —"For the present the labourer thinks that he has a *right* to 2s. 3d. a day in winter, and 2s. 6d. in summer. Next year, perhaps, the labourer will think it *unjust* that he should have less than 4s. a day in winter, and 5s. in summer; and woe to the tyrants who deny him his right!"

"But if they are allowed to fix the labour they are to give and the wages they are to receive—if they are to help themselves, while it lasts, from the whole property of the country, it is too much to expect that they will not prefer idleness, riot, and plunder, to subsistence, however ample, to be earned by toil and hardship." Need we wonder that poor labouring manhood is at a discount in high quarters?

The half million mentioned in connection with the cotton trade applies not only to spinning but to all the branches of labour in the manufacture of cotton, and a further improvement of the productive powers in the cotton trade is included in the calculation that fewer than a hundred thousand human beings could produce as much as ten millions do now.

Money-lending for a consideration is probably as old as society and the use of money, but fortune-making with borrowed money is of recent origin. In olden times it was only people who could not make both ends meet in their household affairs (the hard-ups) who had to resort to borrowing; hence the odium attached to such of the rich as would not lend to neighbours in distress without interest; hence the anathemas of the Primitive Church against usury. A great change has come over the scene. At the present day, borrowing is a source of gain as well as lending. In times of prosperity, when money is easy, large business transactions are carried on by men who have very little property of their own, many of whom make fortunes, and many more who are already rich extend their business operations by the aid of credit, and, as a rule, the opulent make more use of credit than the needy. Mr. Mill, in his happy versatility of entertaining two opinions upon the same subject, denies, under the head of credit as a substitute for money, that credit creates capital. He says:—"As a specimen of the confused notions entertained respecting the nature of credit, we may advert to the exaggerated language so often used respecting its national importance. Credit has a great, but not as many people suppose, a magical, power; it cannot create something out of nothing. How often is an extension of credit talked of as equivalent to a creation of capital, or as if credit were actually capital. It seems strange that there should be any need to point out that credit being only permission to use the capital of another person, the means of production cannot be increased by it, but only transferred. If the borrower's means of production and of employing labour are increased by the credit given him, the lender's are so much diminished. The same sum cannot be used as capital both by the owner and also by the borrower to whom it is lent; it cannot supply its full value in wages, tools, and materials to two sets of labourers at once." One might almost fancy that under credit Mr. Mill understood borrowing and lending between two sets of persons engaged in the same branch of business—the borrowing and lending that frequently takes place among little farmers and tradesmen. If farmer Jones borrow a plough of farmer Brown, it is evident that Brown cannot use the plough while Jones has it. But this borrowing and lending is not credit, and does not come within the province of political economy.

A plough is not a plough at every stage of its existence. When it rests in the warehouse of the agricultural implement maker it is merchandise, the product of a specific kind of labour, and capable of being used in the operation of ploughing as soon as it leaves its resting place—a movement that will take place whenever its purchasing price, or a security equivalent to it, is offered in exchange for it. As long as it rests in the warehouse it is a burden; the utmost it can do by a prolonged stay is to harrow up its possessor's peace of mind, and, perhaps, induce him to slacken his production and discharge some of his workpeople. Now, suppose farmer Brown wants a plough but has no cash to purchase one. If he could only obtain it for hard cash he would have to do without it, and his land would remain barren; but his credit is good. He therefore goes to the manufacturer and buys one, and the manufacturer draws a bill on the transaction, a neighbouring banker discounts it with notes, and by means of these notes the process of ploughmaking is renewed. Now, what has taken place? A few slips of paper in the form of credit have released the plough from the place where it was likely to become a source of embarrassment, and converted it into food-producing capital; they have released a corresponding quantity of the raw materials and tools used in ploughmaking from a similar position; they have given a renewed scope to productive labour and enabled the capitalists to realise their interest and profit. Whose means of production are diminished by this transaction? Is it simply a transfer of capital, or is a capital-creating metamorphosis beneficial to all concerned?

But there is another aspect of our credit system. If farmer Brown could by any contrivance break up the surface of his land, at a trifling expense, equal to ploughing, the saving of the expense of the plough, the horses, and the ploughing would be tantamount to a creation of new capital. The existing paper currency has exactly the same effect compared with a metallic currency. Had the United States been obliged to transact all their business with gold instead of paper, they would have had to part with 140,000,000*l.* worth of produce to purchase the gold requisite to replace the paper in circulation in 1865. By resorting to paper—i.e., credit, they saved (which is tantamount to creating) a capital of equal amount. If our paper currency had to be replaced by gold it would require the whole amount of one year's export of British and Irish produce and manufactures to purchase it, besides an annual wear and tear of more than 350,000*l.* By using paper instead of gold, besides the facilities it affords in the transaction of business, we save the whole amount which the metal would cost us.

The assertion that the same sum cannot supply wages, tools, and materials, to two sets of labourers at once is contrary to established facts, and, as we shall presently see, contrary to Mr. Mill's own statement under another head.

Bifariousness is the very essence of our credit system. The fourteen millions of sovereigns advanced to Government by the Bank of England, maintain their double existence by their paper images, the 14,000,000*l.* bank notes.

As these bank notes are as efficient for productive purposes as their equivalent value in gold, we can come to no other conclusion than that the sum of 14,000,000*l.* of gold may in combination with its intrinsically valueless paper images be made equal to a productive capital of 28,000,000*l.* Now, as all our credit papers are supposed to represent really existing wealth, it is not too much to assert that every sum which enters the charmed circle of credit doubles its power. Mr. Mill states this fact under the head of influence of currency on foreign trade. He supposes that 20,000,000*l.* of gold have been sent abroad and replaced by paper. The effect of this would be in his opinion: —"The value saved to the community by dispensing with metallic money, is a clear gain to those who provide the substitute. They have the use of twenty millions of circulating medium, which have cost them only the expense of an engraver's plate. If they employ this accession to their fortunes as productive capital, the produce of the country is increased and the community benefitted, as much as by any other capital of equal amount. When paper currency is supplied by bankers, the amount is almost wholly turned into productive capital. A banker's profession being that of a money lender, his issue of notes is a simple extension of his ordinary occupation. He lends the amount to farmers, manufacturers, or dealers, who employ it in their several businesses. So employed it yields, like any other capital, wages of labour, and profits of stock. ... The capital itself in the long run becomes entirely wages, and when replaced by the sale of the produce becomes wages again; thus affording a perpetual fund of the value of twenty millions for the maintenance of productive labour, and increasing the annual produce of the country by all that can be produced through the means of a capital of that value." And what becomes of the 20,000,000*l.* of gold while all this is going on? The sum of 20,000,000*l.* of intrinsic value supplies by the aid of its paper images—credit, wages, tools, and materials, to the amount of 20,000,000*l.* to each, of two sets of labourers at once.

X. Profit.

Mr. Mill commences his chapter on profit with the following observation: —"The profits of the capitalist are properly, according to Mr. Senior's well chosen expression, the remuneration of abstinence." It would be an equally well chosen expression to say that rent is the remuneration of land-owning. In my second article I pointed out what difficulties and hardships the employers of labour have to endure to carry on the process of accumulating capital, and shall, therefore, leave my readers to their fate respecting the conclusion as to the remuneration of those difficulties and hardships. But the next statement calls for enquiry. Mr. Mill says: "To popular apprehensions it seems as if the profits of business depended upon prices. A producer or dealer seems to obtain his profits by selling his commodity for more than it costs him; profit altogether, people are apt to think, is a consequence of purchase or sale. It is only (they suppose) because there are purchasers for a commodity, that the producer of it is able to make any profit. The cause of profit is, that labour produces more than is required for its support. The reason why agricultural capital yields a profit, is because human beings can grow more food than is necessary to feed them while it is being grown. Profit arises, not from the incident of exchange, but from the productive power of labour; and the general profit of the country is always what the productive power of labour makes it, whether any exchange takes place or not. If there were no divisions of employments, there would be no buying and selling, but there would still be profit. If the labourers of the country produce 20 per cent. more than their wages, profits will be 20 per cent., whatever prices may or may not be." Before we go any further let us settle what profit means. Profit is a gain resulting from a transaction in which producer and consumer are different persons. To Crassus of ancient Rome, and to Lytton Bulwer's 'Last of the Barons,' a superabundant harvest would have been a real gain; the former could have given more corn to the poor of Rome, the latter could have feasted more retainers;

to both it would have been a source of power. To the modern farmer and landlord it is a source of misery. To the ancient patrician and the feudal baron the gain arising out of production consisted in the quantitative amount of consumables they obtained; to the modern proprietor it consists in the amount of money that can be cleared. The water works of ancient Rome were a great benefit to the people of Rome, but they were no source of profit; the water works of the New River Company are a benefit to the people of London, and a source of profit to the shareholders, because the water has a price; it is sold, and sold for more than it costs to procure it. Profit, then, is a gain resulting from a mode of production under which producers and consumers are two different sets of persons, who have to buy and sell the produce of labour.

According to Adam Smith, rent is the difference between the market price of agricultural produce and the amount of money which satisfies the farmer; David Ricardo has explained from what peculiar circumstances this difference arises.

Mr. Mill has adopted his theory, but does not perceive that profit depends as much on market price as rent. Leaving rent out of the question, what constitutes the farmer's profit? In Mr. Mill's opinion the difference between the quantity of food a man produces and that which is necessary to feed him while he is producing it; in my opinion the difference between the price of labour and the price at which its produce is sold. Whatever this difference amounts to is the amount of the farmer's profit. Let us suppose a young community of families located in some favoured region on a tract of fertile land equally divided among them. They are contented to live on the fruits of their own soil and labour; every family produces by its labour everything required for its subsistence. If they could produce a hundred times as much food as they require it would be of no use, it would be labour in vain. If, after the lapse of some time, another community settled in the neighbourhood on a somewhat poorer soil, but with the same mode of life, it would not make the

74

slightest difference in the social arrangements of the original settlers. A third lot might settle on a still poorer soil without in the least interfering with the other two. If 100, 90, 80 represented the relative fertility of the three different soils, the labour required to procure a subsistence would be in an inverse proportion 8, 9, 10. Suppose these figures to represent hours, the people on the third settlement would have to work ten hours to obtain the same quantity of consumables as the people in the first could obtain in eight. No improvement in the productive powers of either would affect the condition of the others. If the people of No. 3 introduced machinery, by means of which they could produce as much in two hours as formerly in ten, it would make the people of No. 1 neither richer nor poorer than they were before. There being no buying and selling they would still have to produce all they required; the people of No. 3 would produce no more than they required. Will Mr. Mill point out in what direction we are to look for the profit, the remuneration of abstinence arising out of the productive power of the labour of these communities.

Let us now turn from this imaginary state of things to the existing state of society, a state of society in which we have to deal with labourers who can only gain a subsistence by producing things which supply the wants of others, and where they cannot produce for the wants of others without the intermeddling of a capitalist, who exacts a profit. Suppose we represent the productive power of labour by 100, and that, at that rate, the quantity of a given product is exactly equal to the demand, its market price will be equal to its value. If the labouring producer is also the seller there will be neither profit nor loss. If on account of scarcity its price rise 10 per cent, there will be a profit of ten per cent., which may be intercepted by a merchant. If the labourer consumed his own product there would never be any profit; but our labourer works for a capitalist, who is the proprietor of the produce of his labour, and let us take it for granted that he can manage to live on 70; in that case the profit of the capitalist will be 30. Now if Mr. Mill's hypothesis holds good, if profit does not depend on buying and selling, then if by any circumstance the productive power of labour is increased, without a corresponding increase in the rate of wages, the profit of the capitalist will increase in a corresponding ratio. Let us go a step farther. Let us suppose our three communities as having entered the commercial state, and let us apply Ricardo's rent theory to profits. During the period of transition the hours of labour have been equalised, and wages are uniformly at 70. The first produces 100, profit 30; the second 90, profit 20; the third 80, profit 10; total 270, of which 210 are paid in wages, 60 remain as profit. If the productive power of labour increased by 40 per cent. the proportions would be 140, profit 70; 126, profit 56; 112, profit 42, total produce 378; total profit 168. If wages were paid in kind, and the capitalist farmer, like the patrician and baron of old, retained the produce for the use of his own household, it would be a great augmentation of wealth; but the produce has to be sold, it has a price, and its value is estimated in gold. The former proportion of 100 of gold for 100 of produce has not simply changed to 100 gold and 140 produce, but the new proportion is 75 gold to 140 produce. Could the whole of it be sold it would realise 203 of gold; but 180 of the produce is dead stock, its market price is a fiction, therefore only 146 can be obtained. The 168 profit from production is converted into a pecuniary loss of 64, which means bankruptcy, and ruin. If the farmers of the different soils sold their proportionate quantities they would respectively realise 53, 47, 42; their respective losses would be 17, 23, 28. If those of No. 1 could sell their whole they would still clear 5; but those of No. 3, would lose 10. With a reduction of money wages those of No. 1 could continue their farming operations, and even extend them, without any rise of prices, but those of No. 3 would be ruined. So much for profit being independent of prices.

Let us now have a peep at historical realities. The following statements are taken from "Tooke's History of Prices."

"According to Sloane's MSS. a fall of prices occurred between 1617 to 1621, from 43s. 3d. the quarter of eight bushels to 27s.

'Mr. John Chamberlain to Sir Dudley Carleton.

12th February, 1620. We are here in a state to complain of plenty; but so it is, that corn beareth so low a price that tenants and farmers are very backward to pay their rents, and in many places plead disability; for remedy whereof the council have written letters into every shire, and some say, to every market-town, to provide a granary or storehouse, with a stock to buy corn and keep it for a dear year.'

The following was written at the same period: —'England was never generally so poor since I was born as it is at this present, inasmuch that all complain they cannot receive their rents; yet is there plenty of all things but money, which is so scant that country people offer corn and cattle, or whatsoever they have else, in lieu of rent, but bring no money; and corn is at so easy rates as I never knew it to be at, twenty or twenty-two pence a bushel, barley at nine pence, and yet no quantity will be taken at that price.'"

There are similar complaints at subsequent periods of great plenty. During the year 1731-32 and 33 wheat averaged 22s. In a publication by the elder Lord Lyttleton, "Considerations on the Present State of Affairs" (1738), he says, "In most parts of England gentlemen's rents are so ill paid, and the weight of taxes lies so heavy on them, that those who have nothing from the Court can scarce support their families."

Let us now see whether there is any difference in the fate of the farmer and that of the manufacturer. In 1810, the importation of raw cotton was 136,488,935lbs. against 43,605,982lbs. in 1808. The monthly commercial report of the 1st January, 1811, said, "In Lancashire the cotton manufacturers appear, by the late gazettes as well as by private information, to be greatly distressed, and business quite at a stand. In

Manchester and other places houses stop, not only every day, but every hour." The Chancellor of the Exchequer stated shortly after in the House that the large manufacturers had diminished the number of their workpeople by half, the smaller ones had discharged theirs altogether. In 1825 the consumption of cotton was 202,546,863lbs. against 141,038,743lbs. in 1824. November 4th, 1825, a Boston paper stated, "Five mercantile firms failed at New York for 2,500,000 dols." In 1825 Georgia cotton fetched 1s. 6 1/2 d., at the beginning of 1826 it would not sell for 6 1/2 d. In 1845 business was increasing, and prices advancing. There was an increase of 300,000 bales against '44; on the 18th July, 1846, the *Manchester Guardian* stated, "Prices are unremunerative, the millers consider the propriety of working short time." On October 27th, the correspondent of the *Economist* said, "In the course of a fortnight working short time will be more general than at any time since 1825." Thus we see that when the surplus—Mr. Mill's profit—arising out of production is largest, the possibility of turning it to account is smallest. Paradox as it may appear it is, nevertheless, a fact, that in any branch of production, when the produce of labour is largest, poverty and misery are stalking about in its ranks, because the produce has a price, a price which often falls below its labour value, and which cannot be realised except by the sale of the produce. It remains to be proved what connection there is between industrial profits and Ricardo's rent theory. On February 11th, 1847, the correspondent of the *Economist* said, "The difference between the price of raw cotton and yarn was never so small as at present." Feb. 11th, 39 in. 60 reed cloth is sold at 8s. a piece, a ruinous loss to manufacturers. Georgia cotton at that time was from 5d. to 8d. a pound. In 1851, a year of prosperity, the same cotton was sold for 7 3/4 d. in January, and for 5 5/8 d. in July. The same cloth sold for 9s. 7 1/2d. in January, and for 7s. 9d. in July. The highest price up to 1858 was 8s. 6d. How did 8s. become a remunerative price? By increasing the fertility of the instruments of production. The prices that ruled previously to the crisis of 1846 and 1847 were sufficiently remunerative to keep the old machines at work, which carried only from five to six hundred spindles, required six persons to every horse power, and from 8 to 12lbs. of coal per hour per horse power. The improved machines carried a thousand spindles, required only four persons per horse power, and only from 3 1/2 to 4lbs. of coal per hour per horse power. The new machines could produce cotton at a profit, for 8s. a piece, the old ones could not. The proprietors of the fertile machines are in the same position as the farmers on the fertile soil, when corn fell to 75s. and the proprietors of the old ones shared the fate of the farmers on the third soil, they had to give it up. The cause of profit, then, is not the difference between the productiveness of labour and what the labourer can live on. When labour can be hired at a price which is below the market price of the produce of labour, then the employer makes a profit; but the produce must be sold to realise that profit.

XI. Small Farming.

Hitherto I have dealt with theoretical elucidations and conclusions, and negative criticism. I now enter upon, what is commonly called the practical part, the consideration of positive propositions. The measures and means by which Mr. Mill hopes to cure the ills that afflict us, we shall find as unsuitable and impracticable as we found his theoretical conclusions erroneous and contradictory. Instead of discovering a tendency to progressive development, instead of propositions aiming at the regeneration of society, we shall find them obstructive and reactionary, with a deliberate aim towards the attainment of the stationary state. If anyone advocated the old hand-wheel against the modern mule, the handloom against the powerloom, the stage-coach against the railway, he would be looked upon as one labouring under an aberration of mind. Now small farming stands in the same relation to modern farming on a large scale, as hand spinning and weaving to modern machine spinning and weaving. If in former times a man had been in possession of a thousand wheels it would have required a thousand pairs of feet and hands to work them, just as if a thousand persons had possessed a wheel each and worked it in their own homes. In the same way a ten thousand acre estate was cultivated in the same manner as a ten acre farm, there was no difference in the mode of operations, the same amount of manual labour per acre being required on large farms as on small ones. Small farming is the mode of cultivation of the past, it belongs to, and is conformable to a state of society in which almost every household, every village, every province, produces all its own necessaries. It belongs to a state of society in which the great bulk of the population is, as it were, rivetted to the soil, and in which there are few or no chances of getting a living except by the cultivation of the soil. The characteristic distinction between the small working farmer and the large capitalist farmer is, that the former produces food for the consumption of his own family, the latter produces food for the market for the consumption of others. The large farmer is the food producer for an industrial community, the small farmer the food producer for himself. Mr. Mill advocates small farming, but not to the extent of breaking up the existing large farms, he only proposes that "all common land to be brought into cultivation should be devoted to raising up a class of small proprietors." To show what a happy fellow the peasant proprietor is Mr. Mill favours his readers with some French extracts from Sismondi, of which I translate the following choice morsel:—"The peasant who, with his children, does all the work on his little inheritance, who pays no rent to any one above him nor wages to any one below him; who eats his own grain, drinks his own wine, clothes himself with his own hemp and wool, troubles himself little about market prices, for he has little to sell and little to buy, and is never ruined by commercial convulsions. Far from fearing the future he sees it embellishing his hopes; for he puts every moment that is not required for his annual labour to the profit of his offspring for centuries to come. ... He is also eager to buy land at any price. He pays more for it than it is worth, more perhaps than it will return to him." We see at the first glance that there is no room for such a man in a country that boasts of such places as London, Liverpool, and Manchester. For if he wants to be truly happy he will trouble himself as little about the hungry mouths in London, Liverpool, and Manchester as he troubles himself about market prices. If money entice him to produce ought else than what he requires for feeding and clothing his family, he will not be able to furnish it at a reasonable price, since he pays more for his land than it is worth, and on that very account, besides enhancing the price of his produce, necessarily cripples his circulating capital. If such happy beings still existed when Sismondi wrote, I can assure my readers that they have become extinct, since the necessity of money making, and consequently the indispensability of caring about market prices has even penetrated the Alpine regions. The proposal of Karl Burkli, of Zurich (one of the delegates of the International Congress at Geneva), to establish a people's bank for the Canton of Zurich, to enable the peasantry to obtain loans for less than from 5 to 10 per cent. interest is a striking proof of this. But independent of this Mr. Mill himself cites evidence which shows that "the indebtedness of the proprietors in the flourishing canton of Zurich borders on the incredible, so that only the intensest industry, frugality, temperance, and complete freedom of commerce enable them to stand their ground." But the peasantry of Zurich enjoy an advantage which, with the exception of Florentine straw-plaiters, no peasantry in the world enjoys. Mr. Mill states in a foot-note that "four-fifths of the manufacturers of the canton of Zurich are small farmers. The cotton manufacture occupies, either wholly or partially, 23,000 people, nearly a tenth of the population." In the canton of Schaffhausen almost all the landed properties are mortgaged, but rarely for more than half their registered value. And what is the condition of the French peasantry? M. de Veauce stated last year in the Chamber of Deputies that "according to the census of 1851 the mortgages on land amounted to 400,000,000*l.* sterling. Things had become considerably worse for the Government would not publish the returns of 1861." He observed that "if a large estate were for sale in the neighbourhood of a large populated centre, it could be divided into fragments, each of which fetched a high price—but what happened? To buy a mere slip of land men actually borrowed the double of their available capital, looking forward to the future to clear off their debt. Of the 7,846,000 landed proprietors in France, not less than 3,000,000 had been certified by the municipal councils of their communes as being in such a state of absolute destitution that they could pay no personal tax." But the buying of land with borrowed money is not the only way in which the land is mortgaged. Suppose a man leaves at his death nine acres of land, free of debt, and three children, and that the children agree not to claim their three acres each, what happens then? Well, the one who keeps the lot must pay the difference to the other two. And where does he get the money? He mortgages the property, and instead of starting in business with a fund in hand, he starts with a crushing weight of debt, of which he can never rid himself. This and the taxes imposed by the State form the links which chain the peasant to society, and implicate him in the fate of the community. But for these he might be the happy man portrayed by Sismondi, but interest and taxes compel him to sell part of his produce, at all hazards, and generally the best part, leaving the coarsest for himself, and frequently not enough of that.

The life of the peasant is anything but an enviable one. Speaking of the neighbourhood of Zurich Mr. Mill says, "When I used to open my casement, between four and five in the morning, I saw the labourer in the fields; and when I returned from an evening walk, long after sunset, there was the labourer mowing his grass or tying up his vines."

Howitt says about the Germans, "They labour busily, early and late, because they feel that they are labouring for themselves. They plod on from day to day, from year to year, the most patient, untirable, and persevering of animals."

And how does the peasantry fare? Mr. Mill says, "No peasantry on the Continent has the superstition of the English labourer respecting white bread." The Tuscan peasant, according to Sismondi, has but two meals a day in the bad season, "at ten o'clock in the morning he eats his porridge, at nightfall he has soup, and afterwards he has bread with some seasoning. In summer he has three meals, at eight, at one, and in the evening; but he only lights the fire once a day, for his dinner, consisting of soup, afterwards a mess, or salt meat, or dried fish, or beans, or vegetables, which he eats with bread. Salt meat enters but in a very small quantity into his ordinary, for he reckons only 40lbs. of salt pork a year as an ample provision per head; twice a week he puts a little bit into his pottage. Sundays he always has fresh meat, but not more than a pound or a pound and a half, however numerous the family may be." The Flemish farmers and labourers, says Mr. Mill, "live much more economically than the same class in England, they seldom eat meat, except on Sundays and in harvest; buttermilk and potatoes with brown bread is their daily food." Mr. Mill says further, "The peasant proprietors are oftener accused of penuriousness than of prodigality. They deny themselves reasonable indulgences, and live wretchedly in order to economize. In France, among those who, from the hovels in which they live, and the herbs and roots which constitute their diet, are mistaken by travellers for proofs and specimens of general indigence, are numbers who have hoards in leathern bags, consisting of five-franc pieces, which they keep by them perhaps a whole generation, unless brought out to be expended in their most cherished gratification—the purchase of land."

It is admitted that the price of land is far above its value, in Belgium it pays little more than two per cent. Now, if a man does live wretchedly all his life to buy a piece of land, what does it amount to? If he saves 1,000 francs, and buys a piece of land for 2,000 francs, he will get possession of a property, worth perhaps 50 francs a year. As he had to borrow 1,000 francs to pay for his land, and as the money lenders hardly ever lend for less than five per cent., he has to pay 50 francs a year, his own thousand francs bring in as little as the deposit which some of the slop tailors have to leave with their employers. The peasant therefore only works hard and lives hard, and buys land that the mortgagee may realise interest on his money. Mr. Mill maintains that small farming produces more per acre than large farming; but Moreau de Jonnès, in his comparison of England and France, arrives at a different result. According to his calculations in 1850, the annual value of the agricultural produce was:

	France. Francs.	England. Francs.
Per head of the population	133	235
Per cultivator	215	715
Wheat per acre, bushels	18	30

Mr. Mill says, "Large capital applied to farming is, of course, only applied to the very best of the soils of a country. It cannot touch the small unproductive spots, which require more time and labour to fertilize them than is consistent with a quick return of capital." Now, I ask whether it would be good economy in a state of society that boasts of the steam plough to condemn any set of men to cultivate land by superhuman industry; poor land—perhaps with the spade, as in the Walesdistrict—that they may subsist on *buttermilk, potatoes,* and *brown bread.* Yet this is what Mr. Mill proposes to ameliorate the wretched condition of the agricultural labourers. If by any economical arrangement a given product can be produced by less labour than by any other, it is rank folly, and contrary to all sound economy to adopt that which requires most. If the reduction of manual labour is injurious to the poor, that is not the fault of the mode of production, but of the mode of distribution, and it is the business of those who suffer to alter it. The small farm system is condemned, socially and economically. No working men of sound mind will consider the mode of living portrayed by Sismondi and Mr. Mill, combined with the hardships attending it, as an improvement compared with the condition of the British day labourer. But more than that, the continental peasantry turn up their little farms and emigrate. The Germans go wholesale to America, the French flock to the towns, the rural population diminishes, and there is a movement going on of substituting large farming for small farming.

But, there is another aspect of the question. It is now admitted on all sides that co-operation offers the only means for a solution of the labour question. Just as combined and concentrated labour is a superior mode of production to isolated and scattered labour, so co-operative labour is superior to the present mode of production, and must sooner or later supersede it. Co-operative labour is the peculiar child, the natural offspring of factory industry and large farming; co-operation requires a preliminary course of industrial training, and this is the secret why co-operation succeeds better in Manchester than in London. What the London mechanic will do some day from moral conviction the factory labourer does almost from habit. The day labourer on the large farm has had a considerable amount of such training, he is fit to enter upon co-operative farming, the small farmer who is guided by his own whims and caprices is not. To break up the large estates and establish small farming to any extent would be, to say the least, absolutely obstructing the progressive development of agriculture. The working classes have a direct interest to oppose every attempt that may be made in this direction. Instead of converting waste and common lands into small farms the Legislature ought to facilitate their transfer as well as that of the Crown and Church lands to co-operative associations, not as permanent property but on lease, since no private individuals, nor companies with interests separate from the common interests of the people, ought to be invested with the perpetual control and direction of the use of the land—the source of food.

XII. Property.

Mr. Mill says,—"If choice were to be made between communism with all its chances, and the present state of society with all its sufferings and injustices; if the institution of private property necessarily carried with it as a consequence, that the produce of labour should be apportioned, as we now see it, almost in an inverse ratio to the labour—the largest portions to those who never work at all, the next largest to those whose work is almost nominal, and so, in a descending scale, the remuneration dwindling as the work grows harder and more disagreeable, until the most fatiguing and exhausting bodily labour cannot count with certainty on being able to earn even the necessaries of life; if this, or communism were the alternative, all the difficulties, great or small, of communism would be as dust in the balance. But to make the comparison applicable, we must compare communism at its best, with the regime of individual property, not as it is, but as it might be made. The principle of private property has never yet had a fair trial in any country. The social arrangements of modern Europe commenced from a distribution of property which was the result, not of just partition or acquisition by industry, but of conquest and violence.

Individuals need not be chained to an occupation or to a partial locality. The restraints of communism would be freedom in comparison with the present condition of the majority of the human race. The generality of labourers in this and most other countries have as little choice of occupation, or freedom of locomotion, are practically as dependent on fixed rules and on the will of others as they would be on any system short of actual slavery.

The institution of property, when limited to its essential elements, consists in the recognition in each person of a right to the exclusive disposal of what he or she have produced by their own exertions, or received either by gift or by fair agreement, without force or fraud, from those who produced it.

Nothing ought to be treated as property which has been acquired by force or fraud.

When the 'sacredness of property' is talked of, it should always be remembered, that any such sacredness does not belong in the same degree to landed property. No man made the land. It is the original inheritance of the whole species. Its appropriation is wholly a question of general expediency. When private property in land is not expedient, it is unjust. The State is at liberty to deal with landed property as the general interests of the community may require, even to the extent, if it so happens, of doing with the whole what is done with a part whenever a bill is passed for a railroad or a new street. The community has too much at stake in the proper cultivation of the land, and in the conditions annexed to the occupancy of it, to leave these things to the discretion of a class of persons called landlords, when they have shown themselves unfit for the trust. To me it seems almost an axiom that property in land should be interpreted strictly, and the balance in all cases of doubt should incline against the proprietors. The reverse is the case with property in moveables, and in all things being the product of labour; over these the owner's power should be absolute, except where positive evil to others would result from it; but in the case of land, no exclusive right should be permitted to any individual which cannot be shown to be productive of positive good. To be allowed any exclusive right at all over a portion of the common inheritance, while there are others who have no portion, is already a questionable privilege. No quantity of moveable goods which a person can acquire by his labour prevents others from acquiring the same by the same means; but from the very nature of the case, whoever owns land, keeps others out of the enjoyment of it."

The reddest of red communists could not draw a truer, a more abhorrent, and a more strikingly contrasting picture of the social position of the working man and the proprietor, who appropriates the fruits of the working man's toil, than Mr. Mill does; but he contends that this abominable state of society is not a necessary consequence of the institution of private property, and bids us not to judge the regime of individual property as it is, but as it might be made. But what he proposes to eradicate this abomination is only a modification of the laws of inheritance which might have the effect of substituting, in some instances, an exacting and clever trickster for a generous simpleton as inheritor of a fortune, or it might break an annual income of a hundred thousand in two of fifty thousand each. Would this in any way whatever alter the relation between capital and labour? *No! emphatically, no!* It would be an obstruction, and aggravate the case. If all the provisions, all the raw materials, and all the instruments of production requisite to set all the productive labour in motion, were the private property of half a dozen individuals, a parliamentary decree of expropriation would be sufficient to convert all the establishments of production into co-operative concerns. Every invention, every fluctuation that tends to the concentration of the instruments of production in the hands of a few, is a step in advance towards the final and complete emancipation of the working class. As it is, the large manufacturer, the interest of whose capital is sufficient to maintain his household in comfort and affluence, is more likely, when profits run low, to enter into partnership with his workpeople, than the little exacting, avaricious, busy-bodies, who can scarcely hold their ground against the large capitalists, and yearn to make a fortune.

Where, or how, the principle of private property is to have a fairer trial than it has as yet had is beyond my comprehension. In the new world, at all events, there were no feudal restrictions of a bygone age to overcome, and no established church with hereditary prejudices to impede the development, in its full vigour, of the institution of modern private property. The new world was taken possession of by the advanced guard of Europe, by the most robust, the most energetic, and the most advanced—those who preferred braving the dangers and hardships of the wilderness, to submitting peaceably to the social and political fetters of feudalism which cramped and obstructed the march of progress in the old world. They had only a comparatively few defenceless savages to exterminate to make a beginning and have a clear start, and is not the contention between labour and capital as fierce and unrelenting in the new world as in the old? Is the social reformer, the man of new ideas, justified in evading to criticise an institution as it is, by the pretence that it might be made something different?

To deny the 'sacredness' to one kind of private property which is vindicated for another, may have been sound argument at a former period of the world's history, but private property in the products of labour, particularly by the instruments of production, has assumed far too gigantic proportions, and is accompanied by such unsatisfactory relation, that it is hardly worth while to make fish of one and flesh of the other. *"No man made the land,"* therefore, it ought not to be private property. Who made the land, and how is it made at the present moment? The mountain torrents carry the *debris* of the denuded and constantly denuding geological formations over which they pass in suspense, and deposit them as sediments in the low levels, or in the sea. Land, then, is the result of a combination of natural forces; the whole surface of our globe is the result of such combinations; but it is only on the banks of the largest rivers, such as the Nile, the Jordan, the Indus, the Ganges, the Mississippi—the cradles of culture and civilisation—where man can multiply vegetation with little exertion and primitive tools. In less favoured regions a considerable amount of labour is required to prepare the soil for culture; therefore man rendered the land suitable for the production of food. Who makes the moveables, and how are they made? Let us see. John Chinaman takes care of the silkworm, and sends the silk which the insect spins for the good of its offspring to England—a starving Spitalfield weaver converts it into serge. The Australian shepherd tends sheep, and sends their wool, which nature gave the sheep as a protection against wind and weather, to England —a surly and discontended Yorkshireman converts it into cloth. The emancipated negro of Georgia exerts all his ingenuity to obtain a crop of cotton wool, which his employer sends to Liverpool, and the Lancashire operatives convert it into calico. The Russian peasant grows flax, Dundee labourers convert it into linen; and a London tailor, combining all these materials, converts them into a suit of clothes, say for the Duke of Bedford. The suit of clothes, we find, is the result of a combination of natural and social forces. The materials, after having served the purposes for which nature made them, are converted into clothing; and although this process is the work of man, the Duke of Bedford has never moved a finger in this process. He gives the tailor an equivalent, but neither he nor his ancestors have ever done anything to produce that equivalent, and those who produce it—the labourers—have frequently to go short of food and clothing to enable him to give that equivalent. What holds good with the suit of clothes holds good with every other species of property—the result of labour. According to Mr. Mill's own showing, those who work hardest can acquire no property at all, and those who acquire most have the least, or no need at all to work. As to the assertion that "no quantity which a person can acquire prevents others from acquiring the same," this is rank nonsense. The production of materials is limited by the available land necessary for their production. If, with our present means, we can only produce fourteen million suits of clothes a-year for seven millions of male adults, everybody who gets more than two suits deprives others of their share. The late Richard Cobden introduced on one occasion a friend of his to a public meeting who had risen from the ranks, and employed then 4,000 persons. Here, then, is a case where 4,000 hired wages-labourers are required to set the productive machinery of one proprietor in motion. The chances against the labourers ever becoming proprietors are 4,000 to 1. Unless Mr. Mill can show that the great majority of factory operatives have a reasonable prospect of becoming millowners his argument falls to the ground.

As to conquest, the feudal baron had to risk life, and he who was attacked had a chance of defending himself. The modern capitalist need never move off his couch to render his rival's property useless. He has but to give his agents permission to give some clever mechanician a few pounds to improve his machinery, so that he can undersell his neighbour. In the year ending the 31st October, 1853, there were 98 new mills erected in Mr. Horner's district, with an average horse-power of 29; 23 with an average horse power of 12 ceased working. The same movement is still going on. We have seen, in my previous articles, how new inventions, generally introduced by large capitalists, continually render the property of the small capitalists, and the skill of the operative, useless. This is the modem mode of conquest.

Private property in moveables rests upon to better economical foundation than private property in land. No measure of amelioration will effect a cure of the present highly unsatisfactory social relations that does not tend towards the joint ownership of the instruments of production, and nothing but co-operation, the joint ownership of all the instruments of production, can establish an equitable distribution of the produce of labour.

XIII. Wages and Population.

If imposed restraints and restrictions could make the human family wise, virtuous, and happy, the world would have been a paradise long since. Between fashionable and artificial, and wilfully imposed and enforced restraints and restrictions, the great mass of mankind have never been out of the straight jacket yet. Experience, however, has abundantly proved that the more the straight jacket, which has in all ages paralysed the community, is enlarged the better mankind prospers. The restraints and restrictions enforced at various periods against the increase of population form no exception. Men of science tell us that the inherent tendency to propagate and multiply is such, in every species of organism, that any one species, if left unchecked, would in a comparatively short time cover the whole globe; but as this tendency is inherent in all of them, and as the surface of the earth itself conditions a variety, not any single one, either animal or vegetable, has yet succeeded in covering even any extensive tract to the exclusion of all the others. Nature, who is the mother of them all, has provided her own remedy. That the existence of all organic life is limited by the existing means of subsistence, everybody knows. But, when men like Malthus, Mr. Mill, and, I am sorry to add, the editorial staff of the *National Reformer,* apply this principle to the human species, they forget, in the first instance, that, as a rule, the higher organisms feed upon the lower, that the multiplying power increases as organisms descend in the scale, and that man has acquired the means and the power to multiply them according to his need. In the second instance they forsake the path of reason altogether, and under the pretence of applying a scientific principle to the human species, they apply it to a state of society in which the great majority is doomed to suffer privations whatever the existing means of subsistence may be, a state of society that inflicts pecuniary punishment upon the producers whenever they allow full scope to the powers of production. In Malthus and Mr. Mill such a misapplication may be excusable. They trace all the existing misery to overpopulation, and consider the existing order of things in the main as permanently tenable with, and conformable to human happiness; they know no other cure for the ills that afflict society than improving those out of existence who cannot be used, or used up, in the acquisition of wealth for the possessors of all things. In an advanced section of men of progress, like the writers in the *National Reformer,* the advocacy of a doctrine that wrought so much mischief when preached by Pagan and Christian monks of a byegone age, but who, in spite of all their zealous fanaticism, could not divert mankind at large from the ordinary path of nature, is unpardonable. Their very tenets against the established religions imply a mental, a moral, a

92

social, and a political revolution; they imply the dissolution of a state of society in which the right of the labouring man to live is determined by the prospect that others have to use him in acquiring wealth, and the substitution of a state of society in which man has a natural right of his own to live. In all ages, when an established order of things has become untenable, men have doubted the truth of the religion which sanctioned that order of things, and the most material changes in the world have been contended for and established under the banner of vague, abstract beliefs. The antique world, with its slavery and idolatry was defeated, and the feudal system established under the cross. Protestantism defeated the Papacy and the feudal system, and asserted the claims and established the rights of modern private property while pretending to fight simply for the liberty of conscience, and secularism, the protest against all revealed religion is inseparably bound up with the solution of the labour question. To accomplish their historical mission, the secularists must take the spiritual lead of the labour movement, but they cannot do this as long as they endorse and advocate a doctrine, the possible realisation of which is Malthus's and Mr. Mill's last refuge to preserve and perpetuate the rule of capital.

Mr. Mill says: —"It is not generally known in how many countries in Europe direct legal obstacles are opposed to improvident marriages." By the evidence adduced it is certain that Mr. Mill is as ignorant of the causes of those obstacles as the British public is of the obstacles themselves. The dwelling required in the Grand Duchy of Mecklenburg, before a parson will marry a young couple, looks very innocent in an English book, but let us examine what it implies. The surging waves of the first French revolution passed harmlessly by this Eldorado of feudalism. It is but the other day that a Mecklenburg nobleman sentenced a labourer on his estate other house in his, and that the income which sufficed the fathers suffices the children. When this family is formed the exigency of justice and humanity require him to impose the same restraint upon himself to which those who live a life of celibacy submit. A father who has eight children ought to count that six of his children die at an early age, or that six of his contemporaries, and in the following generation three of his sons, and three of his daughters do not marry on account of him."

This is precisely the way in which the continental peasant manages his oxen and cows. As often as one is got ready for the butcher a young one is reared to fill up the place. If there is a good milk cow in the village, the villagers will buy and rear her offspring and sell that of their own cows to be killed. A pretty ideal this of human progress and happiness, to be recommended by one of the greatest sages of the age, to such a community as the industrial working population of the nineteenth century. The state of things for which Sismondi laid down his moral code, is that of Mecklenburg, just described. There are a certain number of cottages to be inhabited, and the number of the rising generation required can be determined with mathematical precision. Everybody is, as it were, chained to the clod on which he was born, the same number that was required, and could subsist a thousand years ago, will be required for ever after. But how are we to apply such regulations to a state of things in which the improvement of the productive powers advances with such rapid strides, as during the last fifty years, and in which the proportionate number of hands required diminishes as rapidly as the means of subsistence, the productiveness of labour increases. Who is to determine, as to who is to have permission to propagate his species and who not. Are we to return to the habit of our Saxon ancestors, and kill the surplus children at their birth, or are human beings to be served like our domestic animals that are not at all, or not any longer required for breeding purposes? What is to be done with the thousands, and hundreds of thousands of adults whose labouring power is superseded by machinery, or who are replaced by children? Who is to determine what number of tailors, shoemakers, etc., will be required twenty years hence? But above all who is to separate the sexes, who is to all intents and purposes to divorce husband and wife after they have two children, and who is to prevent young folks loving each other, because some one has more then two children, and an increase of population would endanger the continuance of the existing state of things? Out upon such humbug; modern society has better and more elevating means to right itself than a cruel immolation on the altar of Moloch.

XIV. Wages and Population.—Continued.

"In the case of the agricultural labourer," Mr. Mill says, "the checks to population may almost be considered as non-existent. The condition of the labourers of some of the most exclusively agricultural counties, Wiltshire, Somersetshire, Dorsetshire, Bedfordshire, Buckinghamshire, is sufficiently painful to contemplate. The labourers of these counties, with large families, and seven, or perhaps eight, shillings for their weekly wages when in full employment, have lately become one of the stock objects of popular compassion; it is time that they had the benefit also of some application of common sense."

Before we proceed with what Mr. Mill calls common sense, let us see what he himself admits under another head. He says, "During the twenty or thirty years last elapsed, so rapid has been the extension of improved processes of agriculture that even land yields a greater produce in proportion to the labour employed." Now, I ask Mr. Mill, are the laws of nature, the inherent tendency to multiply, in the remotest degree connected with the misery of these labourers? The rent of land has as steadily increased as the produce of labour, and the number of labourers required for profit-mongering purposes to raise that produce has as steadily diminished as the general means of subsistence have been augmented. It is the institution which makes the produce of one man's labour the private property of another that is at the bottom of the labourer's misery. It is not his natural fecundity in relation to the latent capabilities of the soil to afford the means of subsistence, nor any defect in the productive power of his labour, nor a deficiency in the actually existing means of subsistence, that makes him wretched, but it is because he lives in a state of society in which much can be produced with comparatively little labour, and in which the welfare of the labourer depends on the cost of production, which assigns less to the labourer in proportion as his labour becomes more productive, that he is wretched.

Now for the common sense, —"Discussions on the condition of the labourers, lamentations over its wretchedness, denunciations of all who are supposed to be indifferent to it, projects of one kind or another for improving it, were in no county and in no time of the world so rife as at present; but there is a tacit agreement to ignore totally the law of wages, or to dismiss it in a parenthesis with such terms as 'hard-hearted Malthusianism,' as if it were not a thousand times more hard-hearted to tell human beings that they may, than that they may not, call into existence swarms of creatures who are sure to be miserable, and most likely to be depraved. Is it true or not that if their numbers were fewer they would obtain higher wages? This is the question, and no other; and it is idle to divert attention from it by attacking any incidental position of Malthus, or some other writer, and pretending that to refute that is to disprove the principle of population." The fault rests entirely with Malthus and his disciples. They alone are responsible for the confusion and complication in which their pet theory is entangled. They have outraged and profaned in a blasphemous manner a scientific principle—that of life being limited by the means of subsistence—and used it as a screen to hide their ignorance of the true basis of all human progress. What is true of a particular class, and under a peculiar phase of social development, they have applied to the whole species; and while ignoring one of the main attributes of the species, they have endeavoured to argue on general grounds that which appertains to a special case. As I have already shown, if by any contrivance ten men could be enabled to produce next year as much wealth for the capitalist as a hundred produce this year, the ten kept at work would receive only a starvation pittance while any of the ninety remained to compete with them. In this case the population would be to the means of subsistence afforded by the rule of capital like 9 to 1. This is the overpopulation in the actual state of society, it is the special case for which the Malthusian proposes to provide a remedy by a restraint upon population, but it is also the special case which all the Malthusians evade to discuss, their arguments being based upon the assumption that the number of labourers required remains the same, that an increase of their numbers only has to be prevented. It is far easier to upbraid and insult parents for having children than to show how nine men out of ten whose labour is considered indispensable to-day, and may become useless to-morrow, can be improved out of existence. However, to answer Mr. Mill's pointed question distinctly, I will declare that it is beyond question that if there was work in any given trade for a thousand men, and only nine hundred do it, they would get more for doing what they could than 1,200 would get for doing it all. But this is all I can admit of his theory. The Malthusian creed rests upon the assumption that society can attain no higher form than that which represents mankind as divided into capitalists and hired wages labourers. The Malthusian therefore is blind to the fact that the existing disorder of things has produced within its own bosom the germ of a superior state of society. He can only see excrescenses and local and accidental irregularities, which he tries to patch up by palliatives. To him anything that threatens the fundamental basis is tantamount to a destruction of all civilisation—of human society itself. Any Malthusian who advocates co-operative self-employment is like a champion of the Divine right of kings advocating constitutional representative self-government; he advocates two causes, of which the complete success of either implies the extinction of the other.

Under the regime of private capital, productive powers have been developed capable of furnishing ample means of subsistence to a more numerous population than that provided for by the existing mode of distribution. Mr. Mill advocates a better distribution and considers a stricter restraint on population, an indispensable means to it. Vain hope! If you restrict the population, you cripple the development of the powers of production. The capabilities of the productive powers and the wants of society, a consequence of the numerical strength of the population—have reached the point at which private ownership in the instruments of production becomes a nuisance, and an obstruction to further progress. Those instruments are the social product of all the preceding generations of the human race. They are the natural inheritance of every living generation, their administration and management is a question of expediency. The regime of capital enables thousands to revel in luxury, without doing anything, brings production to a standstill when millions, able and willing to work, are slowly perishing from want of food. It is a nuisance, an obstruction, away with it. A restraint on population, if such a thing were possible, would render our productive acquisition useless. A further increase of population will burst the shackles and remove the barriers which prevent the living generation from enjoying the inheritance bequeathed by its ancestors. So much for the special case.

Mr. Mill continues: —"Is it not allowed on both sides, that in old countries, population presses too closely upon the means of subsistence?" *I say, No!* To compare Great Britain as it is with the United States or Australia, as they are under the occupation of Europeans, who use the same appliances that are used in a country, the inhabitants of which have acquired them during the successive stages of development from barbarism to the highest known state of civilization and density of population —is shifting the question, and amounts to a shuffle. To prove the Malthusian theory it must be demonstrated that the ancient Britains, the Anglo Saxons, the Aborigines of America and Australia, possessed ampler means of satisfying their wants than we do. Let us hear Professor Senior's opinion: "The state of savage nations is a state of habitual poverty and occasional famine. A scanty population, and scantier means of subsistence. If a single country can be found in which there is now less poverty than is universal in a savage state, it must be true that, under the circumstances in which that country has been placed, the means of subsistence have a greater tendency to increase than the population.

If it be conceded, that there exists in the human race a natural tendency to rise from barbarism to civilization, and that the means of subsistence are proportionately more abundant in a civilized than in a savage state, and neither of these propositions can be denied, it must follow that there is a natural tendency in subsistence to increase in a greater ratio than population.

All that degrades the character, or diminishes the productive power of a people, tends to diminish the proportion of subsistence to population and *vice versa*. And, consequently, that a population increasing much more rapidly than the means of subsistence is, generally speaking, a symptom of mis-government indicating deeper seated evils, of which it is only one of the results." I entirely endorse this opinion.

Fifty years ago Malthus pointed with horror to China as an over populated country where people sold their daughters, killed their new born children, and in times of scarcity, sold themselves into slavery to procure food. China was then about eight times as large as France, and had a population of 330,000,000; a population of 41,625,000 in France would be equally dense, and is nearly reached. How does modern France fare? In 1760 the consumption of wheat amounted to 108 litres per head; in 1784, to 125; under the first empire to 133, and since 1840, to 175, the population has more than doubled during that time. It is therefore not want of space that cripples the means of subsistence in China, but it is an obsolete and barbarous mode of production, antiquated social, political, and proprietary arrangements, tolerated by a degenerating race, that cripples the resources. During the 17th century nearly every second year was a year of dearth; during the 18th every 3rd;

during the 19th every 4th; over the whole of Europe.

According to the last returns of the Board of Trade, the density of the population in the different countries is, per square mile: United Kingdom 258; Italy 225; France 180; Prussia 179; Austria 155; Spain 84; Russia in Europe 31; Turkey 19; United States 11. The Turks occupy one of the fairest regions of Europe, and if the scientific part of the Malthusian population theory were correct, the Turks would be the best provided nation of Europe, we know they are the worst by far. Four hundred years ago, when the Europeans first set foot upon America, the red Indians suffered from famine and all the calamities and diseases inseparable from famine. Four hundred years the Europeans have poured in and multiplied at a rapid rate, but there is now no fear of famine except from social causes.

XV. Wages and Population.—Concluded.

Of the popular remedies for low wages, Mr. Mill says: —"The simplest expedient which can be imagined for keeping the wages of labour up to the desirable point, would be to fix them by law. Some have proposed to fix a minimum. Another plan which has found many advocates among the leaders of the operatives, is to form local boards of trade, and promulgate a rate of wages based upon natural equity, not upon the state of the labour market. Others think the employers ought to give sufficient wages, and if they do not willingly, should be compelled by general opinion."

"Popular sentiment looks upon it as the duty of the rich, or of the state to find employment for all the poor. If the moral influence of opinion does not induce the rich to spare from their consumption enough to set all the poor to work at 'reasonable wages,' it is supposed to be incumbent on the state to lay on taxes for the purpose, either by local rates, or votes of public money. The proportion between labour and the wages fund would thus be modified to the advantage of the labourers, not by restriction of population, but an increase of capital." "If this claim on society could be limited to the living generation; if nothing more were necessary than a numerous accumulation, sufficient to provide permanent employment at ample wages for the existing numbers of the people; such a proposition would have no more strenuous supporter than myself."

"But it is another thing altogether, when those who have produced and accumulated are called upon to abstain from consuming until they have given food and clothing, not only to all who now exist, but all whom these or their descendants may think fit to call into existence. Such an obligation acknowledged and acted upon, would suspend all checks, both positive and preventive; there would be nothing to hinder population from starting forward at its rapidest rate; and as the natural increase of capital would, at least, not be more rapid than before, taxation, to make up the growing deficiency, must advance with the same gigantic strides. The attempt would of course be made to exact labour in exchange for support. But experience has shown the sort of work to be expected from the recipients of public charity. When the pay is not given for the sake of work, but the work found for the sake of the pay, inefficiency is a matter of certainty; to exact real work from day labourers without the power of dismissal, is only practicable by the power of the lash." "But let them work ever so efficiently, the increasing population cannot increase the produce proportionally: the surplus, after all were fed, would bear a less proportion to the whole produce and to the population: and the increase of the people going on in a constant ratio, while the increase of produce went on in a diminishing ratio, the surplus would in time be wholly absorbed; taxation for the support of the poor would engross the whole income of the country; the payers and the receivers would be melted down into one mass. The check to population either by death or prudence, could not then be staved off any longer, but must come into operation suddenly and at once; every thing which places mankind above a nest of ants or a colony of beavers, having perished in the interval."

"Every one has a right to live. We will suppose this granted. But no one has a right to bring creatures into life, to be supported by other people."

"It would be possible for the state to guarantee employment at ample wages to all who are born. But if it does this, it is bound in self-protection, and for the sake of every purpose for which government exists, to provide that no person shall be born without its consent. If the ordinary and spontaneous motives to self-restraint are removed, others must be substituted. Restrictions on marriage, at least equivalent to those existing in some German states, (three cheers for Mecklenburg) or severe penalties on those who have children when unable to support them, would then be indispensable."

This is the *common sense* of the most celebrated of all the political economists of established celebrity. Reader! you who know Mr. Mill's political economy only by the praises bestowed upon it by the capitalist press, do you not feel an inkling to start and announce this gospel of salvation to all who have been deprived of employment in consequence of the crisis of 1866, and tell them that their parents are at the root of the evil for having brought them into life without previously insuring them the means of subsistence, and that they in their generation are worse than criminals for persisting in the same course after Malthus and his great prophet have laid down the golden rule for human happiness? It is clear that Mr. Mill's social philosophy has not yet passed the boundaries of the 43rd of Elizabeth and the parish stoneyard and oakum room substituted by the poor law of the liberal Parliament in 1834. It is the nakedest and most misanthropic expression of the proprietarian and utilitarian point of view of the natural right of man to live. It sanctions the arrogation of capitalists to claim all the produce of labour as their absolute and exclusive private property, and treats that portion which must be surrendered without an increased return towards the maintenance of the producers as public charity. Remember the Stockport spinners! Was the improved machinery, purchased, between 1840 and 1843 by the millowners, with the profits made out of the labour of the 800 spinners who were previously employed at 1*l*. 2s. a week, and the fact that after the establishment of the improved machinery, the 140 spinners, working three times the number of spindles they had previously worked, for 13s. a week, a test that they were morally disqualified to bring children into life? Or was it a test that with increased facilities to give employment to the poor, the accumulation of the prerequisites of production would remain stationary, or that increased production would progressively diminish the productive power of labour? Has the labourer who has procured the means of subsistence for an increased and increasing population, no natural claim, no moral claim, no claim of any kind to its benefits, save the bone of contention, and the moral struggle for existence which those who deprive him of the fruits of his toil vouchsafe for his lot? Is he to be visited with severe penalties for having children, while others revel in the luxuries which he produced? Who brings creatures into life, to be supported by other people, the poor? Never! They support their own and other people's too. The rich do not even grant their offspring the food which nature has provided for it, the mother's milk. The women of the poor and the cows have to replace the mothers of wealthy infants, and the poor have to nurse them, find food, clothing, shelter, and amusement for them into the bargain when they grow up. Then punish the rich for begetting children. Send every lady who does not suffer from bodily infirmity, who refuses to do the natural duty of a mother to her child, to a nunnery; and every gentleman who becomes a father without adding to the stock of the consumables of the community into solitary confinement on workhouse fare.

Mr. Mill asks next: —"By what means, then, is poverty to be contended against? How is the evil of low wages to be remedied? If the expedients usually recommended for the purpose are not adapted to it, can no others be thought of? Is the problem incapable of solution? Can political economy do nothing, but only object to everything, and demonstrate that nothing can be done?

All experience shows that the mass of mankind never judge of moral questions for themselves, never see anything to be right or wrong until they have been frequently told it; and who tells them that they have any duties in the matter in question, while they keep within matrimonial limits? Who meets with condemnation, or rather, who does not meet with sympathy and benevolence, for any account of evil he may bring upon himself and those dependent on him, by this species of incontinence? While a man who is intemperate in drink, is discountenanced and despised by all who profess to be moral people, it is one of the chief grounds made use of in appeals to the benevolent, that the applicant has a large family and is unable to maintain them." To this the following foot-note is appended: —"Little improvement can be expected in morality, until the producing of large families is regarded with the same feeling as drunkenness or any other physical excess." —One would imagine that children were rained down upon married people, direct from heaven, without their being art or part in the matter; that it was really, as the common phrases have it, God's will and not their own, which decided the numbers of their offspring.

"But let us try to imagine what would happen if the idea became general among the labouring class, that the competition of too great numbers was the principal cause of their poverty, so that every labourer looked (with Sismondi) upon every other who had more than the number of children which the circumstances of society allowed to each, as doing him a wrong —as filling up the place which he was entitled to share. Any one who supposes that this state of opinion would not have a great effect on conduct, must be profoundly ignorant of human nature; can never have considered how large a portion of the motives which induce the generality of men to take care even of their own interest, is derived from regard for opinion— from the expectation of being disliked or despised for not doing it." Mr. Mill winds up with stating that, "If a prudent regulation of population be not reconcilable with the system of hired labour, the system is a nuisance, and the grand object of economical statesmanship should be to bring the labouring people under the influence of stronger and more obvious inducements of this kind of prudence, than the relations of workmen and employers can afford."

The grand remedy is to transport at once a considerable fraction of the youthful agricultural population to the colonies, at the public expense; the other is to raise small proprietors, the proposition already alluded to. Lest there should be any doubt as to the reactionary tendency of these remarks, let us see what the great Reformer says two years later, towards the end of the second volume. "If it were evident that a new hand could not obtain employment but by displacing or succeeding to one already employed, the combined influence of prudence and public opinion might generally be relied on for restraining the coming generation within the numbers necessary for replacing the present.

I cannot therefore regard the stationary state of capital and wealth with the unaffected aversion so generally manifested towards it by the political economists of the old school."

There you have the quintessence of what you have to expect in the shape of progress if you hand your affairs over to the custody of the new (?) school, originally established by Parson Malthus and adopted in the lump by John Stuart Mill. Only fancy what a pleasant life it would be if human nature could be so far degraded and debased as to look upon a pregnant woman with the same disdain as upon a drunken harlot lying in the gutter, or treat an honest man with a large family of little children in distress in the same manner as a drunken vagabond asking for alms; or to be down upon the children of your neighbour like the hens in a farmyard when they get a stranger among them, according to the precepts of Sismondi.

One necessary accompaniment to such a moral code would be some visible sign, easily distinguishable, to inform strangers whether a woman was pregnant with or without the consent of the authorities, that she might be treated accordingly. For schoolmasters and schoolmistresses none would be better qualified than old maids and old bachelors who had been disappointed in love and cordially hated the opposite sex. They would also be the best magistrates and legislators. Happily humanity has rejected similar teachings at a time when there was far less prospect of making life comfortable than there is now, and when eternal salvation was held out as a reward instead of the questionable luxury of improved wages-slavery for the many, and the undisturbed possession of unbounded wealth by the few. Mr. Mill seems to be credulous enough to believe that an opinion can be created to curb the most indomitable instinct, inherent in all organic life, but he requires the lash to make people work to sustain life in ease and comfort. The opinion of one's fellow men counts for nothing here. Is there no possibility of finding employment for people in distress, but on the plan of the stone-yard and the oakum-room? Is it not possible that at no very distant date the working class will have sufficient power in Parliament to do for itself what the landowners are doing now under the Land Improvement Act, obtain credit to extend self-supporting co-operative labour? Is it not remarkably strange that Mr. Mill should, among his popular remedies, not so much as allude to the most popular of all, and the one that is the peculiar child of modern industry, the one that was first demanded by the factory operatives of Lancashire more than fifty years ago—I speak of the reduction of the number of the hours of labour. This is the measure of progress which will to some extent equalise the supply of, and the demand for, labour; on its progress and success depends the social, the mental, and moral elevation of the working class; on its success depends the progress of co-operative self-employment—it will march apace with it. It is the measure which, as far as it has been carried, has fulfilled all that was expected from it, and it is also the measure which, as Professor

Fawcett (to his honour be it said) has several times pointed out in the House, will ere long bring some of us manhood suffrage advocates to loggerheads with some of our present political allies, and bring us into friendship with the Tories. I have much more to say on this point, but must reserve it for a future occasion.

And now a few words about the stationary state. If the tendency to multiply is inherent, a stationary state is unnatural, and can only precede a positively declining state. If at any of the numerous stages of the development of the human species it had been possible permanently to arrest the increase of population, and hinder it from overstepping the existing limits of the means of subsistence, even prospectively, that moment would have been the end of all human progress, and it will be the end of all human progress whenever that moment arrives. Had the wiseacres of the Stone period succeeded in limiting the number of families to the number of the stone caves provided by nature, no building trades would ever have troubled the world, no tailors would be required, man, like his step-brother, the ape, would be confined to certain geographical latitudes. As it is, the rebels, the unruly multitude, have never cared much for established notions, and hence the great mass of mankind has plodded on in happiness, and grief, and woe, frequently with bloody heads, in search of a higher destiny. The race has incessantly advanced, but the same section was not always at the head. Each particular epoch produced the germ, the foundation for a superior state of things, though the nations that produced it resigned the lead. Asia Minor and Egypt, the mothers of the civilisation of ancient Greece, resigned the lead to ancient Greece; Greece in her turn produced the civilisation of Rome, and resigned the lead to Rome; Rome succumbed to the Teutonic barbarians, they gathered up the *debris* of the empire they had sacked, became Christians, and established the feudal state upon its ruins. From that moment until the present hour the lead has remained with the descendants of those barbarous Teutons. The feudal state produced a revolutionary class within its own bosom, which destroyed the work of its ancestors, and established the modern state upon the ruins; the modern state has produced a revolutionary class, the modern working class, which has all the required energy, tact, and courage to subvert, in its turn the institutions of its predecessors, and establish a superior state of things upon the very same spot.

Since the Thirty Years' War the Anglo-Saxon branch of the Teutonic family has acquired the lead; during the present generation the American offshoot has entered into competition. Old *Germania* has been asleep for many a year, but she is rapidly shaking off her shackles to come to the rescue; the sons of France are only lurking in ambush ready for a call; but if John Bull should prove unworthy of the lead, and does not quickly clear the Augean stable of all the antiquated filth that has gathered about him, and threatens a serious interruption to the further increase of population, if he listens to the advice of Mr. Mill and his abettors, Brother Jonathan is sure to snatch the lead from him, and deprive Old England and the rest of the Old World of the honour of marching arm in arm with him to the emancipation of the human race.

During the whole course of history not a single tribe or nation can be cited that remained progressive with a stationary population; we cannot remain progressive now if we put more restraints on population than those we cannot avoid. With the means of production at present known, this country could produce food for four times its present inhabitants, and human nature will burst the chains of wages-slavery, and scatter proprietory rights to the winds before it will submit to self-immolation to sustain an untenable state of stagnation and misery.

www.ingramcontent.com/pod-product-compliance
Lightning Source LLC
Chambersburg PA
CBHW070200290526
45789CB00002B/855